Third Edition

ASSIGNING,
RESPONDING,
EVALUATING

A WRITING TEACHER'S GUIDE

Third Edition

ASSIGNING, RESPONDING, EVALUATING

A WRITING TEACHER'S GUIDE

——————— ≪≫ ———————

Edward M. White

CALIFORNIA STATE UNIVERSITY,
SAN BERNARDINO

ST. MARTIN'S PRESS

New York

Senior English editor: Karen Allanson
Development editor: Kristin Bowen
Managing editor: Patricia Mansfield Phelan
Project editor: Amy Horowitz
Cover design: Sheree Goodman

Library of Congress Catalog Card Number: 94-65194

Manufactured in the United States of America.

9   8   7   6
f   e   d   c   b

For information, write:
St. Martin's Press, Inc.
175 Fifth Avenue
New York, NY 10010

ISBN: 0-312-10217-8

PREFACE

Some educators feel that evaluation in general and testing in particular have little to do with teaching and learning. Composition instructors have good grounds for feeling that way, in light of the many abuses and misuses of testing in American schools, especially in writing programs. Many writing tests are imposed from outside the classroom by administrators unfamiliar with the teaching situation and are scored in more or less mysterious ways. The widespread use of multiple-choice mechanics and usage tests as if they were writing assessments distorts the teaching of writing from earliest schooling through many university programs. And test results are routinely used to support or suggest incompetence on the part of the students, the teachers, or both. It is no wonder that so many of those teaching in American schools—from first-grade teachers wondering about the mechanisms that might prevent some children from getting into second grade to college professors seeing their best students attempting to pass graduate record or law school entrance examinations—consider evaluation the enemy of learning. Teachers of writing in particular, charged in part with the responsibility for supporting the creativity and individuality of their students, normally resist evaluation and the effects of grading on their students.

At the same time, everyone knows that some sort of evaluation is crucial for learning ("How'm I doing?"), and most teachers of writing spend many hours a week grading papers in an attempt to help students write better. Clearly, despite their usual dislike of grading, writing instructors need and use evaluation to do their jobs. Some kinds of evaluation are obviously more valuable—and less offensive—than others.

Let's distinguish, in the first place, two general purposes for evaluation: (1) evaluation as an administrative sorting device, to make institutions more efficient, more accountable, and more objective, and (2) evaluation as a personalized teaching device, to help students learn more effectively. Not all evaluation devices fall neatly into these categories, of course, and some of the most useful are able to work at both the institutional and the personal level. For instance, a good placement test is institutionally efficient because it arranges students in convenient teaching groups and is also valuable for instructors because it gives them relatively homogeneous groups to work with. But most of the testing devices that rightly bother postsecondary writing teachers have both strict institutional purposes and negative effects on students: proficiency tests designed to identify failures, admission tests to screen out the unprepared, "value-added" tests to convince legislators that students have accumulated information, and the like. Such tests have little to do with the teaching of writing. When teachers are forced to choose between tailoring their teaching to an inappropriate institutional test and helping their students learn how to write, they are bound to consider evaluation an intrusion into the classroom.

My concern in this book is largely with the second purpose, evaluation as a way of helping students learn more effectively. Because part of such evaluation includes giving reliable, fair, and valid tests, I will suggest some ways in which these evaluation devices can support institutional goals, such as placement or outcome assessment. But our primary concern is personal: How can evaluation help the teacher help the student? Further, this book is designed to accomplish that task while saving the instructor time and labor. Readers of earlier editions will notice, however, the increased space given to institutional assessment in this edition, a reflection of the increasing external pressures on writing classes and, indeed, all education.

Although this book is addressed generally to all who teach writing or use writing in their courses, it often speaks directly to those teaching first-year students in American colleges and universities, responsible for instructing over a million students a year in rhetoric and composition. I do not intend to exclude either high school teachers (whose honors and advanced placement courses are often at a higher level than many college composition courses), teachers of advanced composition courses, or those involved in writing across the curriculum programs. In fact, all of us face the same problems of developing worthwhile writing assignments, responding sensitively to what students write, and evaluating that work intelligently and fairly.

The first chapter opens with a series of concrete and practical suggestions about constructing and giving writing assignments—a topic not usually attended to in the training of teachers of college writing courses despite its being the crucial first stage in working with student writers. The focus is on the development of clear topics for a wide variety of purposes and student populations. The sample assignments present a variety of successful topics that call for specific skills in the context of the writing course. Each assignment is followed by a brief discussion ("Tips for Teaching and Scoring") that is designed to help with prewriting instruction, class use of the topic, and evaluation.

The second chapter focuses on the immediate practical problems of giving and responding to essay tests. Teachers who take the time to work through this material with their students will earn enduring gratitude, for nowhere else will students encounter systematic help with these problems; at best, some students will pick up versions of these ideas from their friends or from a counselor. An additional advantage to instructors is that by seeing essay tests from the students' point of view (how quickly we forget!), we can avoid the most common problems and construct better tests than those we took as students—and thereby elicit better writing from our students.

The third chapter presents two diagnostic writing tests based on personal experience. The fourth chapter proposes two additional diagnostic writing tests based on analysis of given texts. These tests can serve at least two purposes: Used in the classroom, they will help the course get under way with interesting writing assignments, and institutionally they will provide information for placement of students in appropriate writing classes. Each assignment is followed by some sample student essays at different levels of performance and by scoring guides for consistent grading. Instructors who give pretests and posttests to their classes can use these assignments for that purpose; the chapters include some discussion of the assignments and the best ways to use them for "outcome assessment." (This behaviorist concept, sometimes supplemented by the commercial metaphor "value-added testing," argues that any kind of learning must yield a statistically significant improvement in test scores.) Most teachers will find that these assignments (all of which have been developed and used successfully both on tests and in college freshman composition classrooms) are good ways to help their students do college-level writing. The topics are appropriate, with clear demands, and are interesting to most first-year students; they allow students to examine their own writing processes and to make entries in their writing logs; they are relatively easy to grade (using the scoring guides), will allow for direct diagnosis of writing problems, and can lead to useful conferences with students.

Chapter 5 is new to this edition and focuses on the two most difficult and controversial uses of writing assessment in higher education: placement in the first writing course and certification of writing ability to meet college and university requirements. Although both are institutional issues, writing instructors are usually involved in the development and administration of the assessments that result. Their nature and content have a profound effect on the goals and curricula of writing courses as well as on the standards and climate of the entire institution.

Chapter 6 turns to a sorely neglected matter, responding to student writing. Responding means much more than grading, just as grading means much more than marking errors. In recent years, studies of responding patterns have taught us much about what is useful—and not useful—to say to students about their written work. This chapter attends to new options for responding, such as peer reading, and to new reading theories, which suggest that the reading of texts (including student texts) is more complicated than we used to think it was.

Chapter 7 turns to a means of assessment familiar in the fine arts and adapted to writing courses in recent years: portfolios. These collections of materials offer additional instructional and assessment options to instructors and have a greater scope than any other method for valid institutional assessments that support classroom teaching. But they are still fraught with problems and difficulties. While offering practical suggestions on the use of portfolios, this chapter summarizes the accumulated experiences that writing instructors and writing programs have had with portfolios.

Assigning, Responding, Evaluating offers teaching faculty a new kind of support for the writing class. It is not a mere collection of tests and assignments, though it includes both, but is rather an evaluation guide based on writing and reading theory and integrally related to the teaching of writing. It is designed to help the teacher evaluate writing in a consistent and explainable way and to help as well in the creation of, use of, and response to writing assignments.

ACKNOWLEDGMENTS

Without the encouragement and advice of Andrea Lunsford and Robert Connors, this book would never have been begun. Karen Allanson, Kristin Bowen, and Amy Horowitz of St. Martin's Press have encouraged this ambitious third edition. I must also thank the many colleagues who have worked with me on various testing projects, including the California State University Freshman English Equivalency Examination and the pilot essay project of the Medical College Admissions Test, for ideas that have worked their way in some form into this book.

Finally, I would like to offer thanks to Alexandra Babione of Southern Illinois University at Edwardsville, Lynn Z. Bloom of the University of Connecticut, Elizabeth Burris of Stanford University, Michael Flanigan of the University of Oklahoma, Karen Greenberg of the City University of New York, Christine Hult of Utah State University, Eugene Soules of Sonoma State University, and Linda Woodson of the University of Texas at San Antonio. Their thoughtful reviews and comments guided this revision in many matters, large and small.

Edward M. White

CONTENTS

C H A P T E R   4
Placement or Diagnostic Essay Tests Based on Given Texts   73

C H A P T E R   5
Exit and Proficiency Assessments   99

EPILOGUE
**Concluding Notes on Assessment and the Teaching
of Writing   165**

Third Edition

ASSIGNING, RESPONDING, EVALUATING

A WRITING TEACHER'S GUIDE

CHAPTER 1

WRITING ASSIGNMENTS AND ESSAY TOPICS

⬦

Devising writing assignments for students in writing courses is one of the most taxing and least understood parts of any teacher's job. There is no escaping this task, not even if we believe that students should select their own topics. That just shifts the difficult job of selecting assignments to the students, who themselves need much help in figuring out what to write about and how. Besides, there must be some kind of curriculum in any course, which in turn suggests that certain things are to be learned at different points in the course. Some kinds of writing, some kinds of topics, will suit the curriculum better than others. Which? The teacher must decide.

We need to keep in mind that the writing of topics is, after all, *writing*. All the problems and all the stages of writing are part of the process of devising topics, and no one should imagine it to be easy. The extraordinary compression of the form, the need for clarity and exactness of communication, the requirement that topics elicit a response from a range of students with disparate interests and varying levels of creativity, and the pressures of grading and the curriculum all add to the unique difficulty of the writing of writing topics. It is no wonder that most attempts fall short. Yet we must offer the best assignments we can devise to stimulate our students' creativity and willingness to learn

1

what we teach. This chapter suggests some concepts to guide the development of writing assignments, followed by a series of examples.

CONSTRUCTING WRITING ASSIGNMENTS

Planning Assignments for Discovery and Revision

Writing courses should undermine the night-before, all-night typing frenzy in which many student essays are produced. Sometimes known as the McPaper, this fast-food version of writing offers little nutritional value to students and is frequently indigestible for readers. Although the pattern is more prevalent outside of composition courses, it is a strong enough pattern that students are likely to use it unless the assignment makes it impossible. Few students really expect, as they begin college, to produce more than one draft of an essay; many students tend to feel that the first draft is a fully formed text, to be changed as little as possible. Even good students will, at most, retype an initial draft with an eye to neatness, spelling, and footnote format—the primary criteria for good grades according to folklore (and much experience).

Because virtually all professional writers spend substantial amounts of time revising their work, the designers of useful writing courses—and of writing assignments in all courses—should follow that model and recognize the importance of revision by seeking to establish new patterns for both students and teachers that emphasize revision. The most effective writing assignments set up a continuum of drafting and revising that begins when the assignment is distributed and concludes at the end of the term—if then.

Sequencing Writing Assignments

Most students experience writing assignments as a series of discrete tasks with little overlap. Many writing courses are actually designed so that the assignments are unrelated—a narrative followed by a comparison/contrast paper, analysis of a poem followed by analysis of a short story. Even teacher comments on papers, which are intended to lead to improvement on later work, may only affect revisions of the same paper as the student turns to new and apparently unrelated tasks.

If writing assignments can be sequenced so that each one builds directly on the one before it, students are likely to incorporate revision into their writing process and produce better work. If revisions on the present paper can be included as part of the next paper, they will seem a natural part of the writing process, and the instructor's comments will appear as helpful suggestions for the task to come rather than as judgments to be filed away or disregarded. If entries in a writing journal can lead to class papers, both the journal and the papers will seem related as parts of the overall writing process. Similarly, if readings can be sequenced, the reading that students do will have texture and context and will resemble the academic reading that students will do elsewhere.

One way to sequence assignments is to subdivide a complex task so that it can be approached as a series of smaller jobs. Some customary writing assignments embed a sequence of subtasks, and unpacking those subtasks can help the instructor as well as the student understand all the steps involved. For example, a comparison/contrast paper calls for a series of tasks and skills, each of which could be the focus of a separate assignment: (1) Summarize text A. (2) Summarize text B. (3) List similarities and differences between texts A and B. (4) Write an essay in which you develop an idea about the similarities and differences between texts A and B.

The complexity of the comparison/contrast paper makes many teachers unwilling to assign it, for such writing is rare outside the classroom and students require substantial help in understanding its demands. Yet its very complexity is attractive to some teachers of advanced students, who are ready to rise to its challenge when it is part of a coherent sequence. If a class is working with summaries and book reviews, a good assignment might ask students to compare and contrast two reviews from different kinds of publications (say, a newspaper or a popular magazine and a scholarly journal) of the same book. As students work through the sequence of subtasks, they learn about differences in media, audiences, and assumptions as they construct their own essays. The next assignment might call for the writing of a book review to be submitted to a particular publication.

Similarly, an assignment to write about an important event from childhood could be approached as a series of steps, each building on the one before: (1) describe the setting of the event, using clear and vivid detail; (2) narrate the event chronologically, combining the story with its setting; (3) speculate about why the event stays in the mind, why it remains significant to the writer and why it might become interesting to the reader; (4) narrate the event, rearranging it so that significance rather than chronology becomes the organizing feature;

(5) revise the writing so that the meaning of the event is shown, embedded in the narration, rather than (or as well as) told.

Another example of sequencing assignments could emerge from a focus on the skills that need to be developed for a complex paper. The last sample assignment in this chapter is a research paper, which demands a series of skills from the writer, each of which could be at the center of a separate assignment. A single-source assignment (such as the one given on page 19) will help students understand the most difficult problem for a research paper: incorporating someone else's ideas into one's own writing as support (rather than replacement) for one's own idea. Most students simply insert quotations without comment or connection into their texts, and students need to learn ways to use this kind of evidence before they can handle research; the concept can be learned by writing and revising a single-source paper.

Before a student can complete a research paper successfully, other separate skills are required, and a series of assignments could focus on each of them. Research requires library and on-line search skills, which can and probably should be taught separately as students begin their research. Even advanced college students have problems with summarizing and evaluating sources; short assignments on sources are appropriate after research has gotten under way. Most students are entirely unaware of scholarly journals and their important role in developing knowledge, so assignments that lead students into these journals will help them understand and join in academic discourse. An underlying problem for many students is to find ideas of their own to pursue and develop in the face of all the authoritative source materials they have discovered; an assignment asking them to write about differing interpretations of the same material will help them find their own topics and their own voices.

Another opportunity for sequencing writing assignments will emerge from a designed sequence of reading assignments. Because so many writing instructors are graduates of literature programs, the usual writing curriculum centers on a series of reading assignments, with the writing assignments appended to the reading. Often these reading assignments are more or less random. But a more effective writing course would be based on a sequenced series of writing assignments designed to help students attain a clear set of goals, with the readings serving as models and stimulation for those assignments. The reading in a course could present a series of fictions moving from simple narratives to postmodern stories with the narrator interwoven with the characters; writing assignments on narrative point of view could increase in complexity with each selection, perhaps moving toward postmodern personal essays themselves.

Writing Assignments Presented in Written Form

After planning the assignment, the next step in eliciting good writing from students is the distribution of a written assignment. Many teachers fail to hand out such assignments, simply telling the class what they want or jotting something on the chalkboard to be copied (or miscopied). Such casual treatment of the assignment suggests that a similarly casual response is called for. Even a written and discussed assignment can lead to misunderstanding by students; less careful assignments routinely lead to confusion. "Oh," the student will say, "I didn't remember what you wanted." Many experienced teachers have learned that they must write out, distribute, and discuss their assignment directions if they are to be taken seriously.

Some teachers prefer to let students choose their own subjects for writing, on the grounds that such openness will encourage creativity and a greater sense of ownership of the topic. With undefined topics, however, a large part of the student's energy available for writing must go into selecting, defining, and redefining a topic. If more than one or two such exercises are included in the writing course, students have less opportunity to learn other aspects of the writing processes, such as development and demonstration of ideas, use of sources, and revision. Open topics, in my experience, are more likely to reflect an unclear and problematic course design than a commitment to independent and creative thought; such topics are also an open invitation to the unscrupulous to purchase ready-made essays, which are widely available.

Despite these problems, some superior writing instructors remain committed to open assignments; they are convinced that students will write better when they are free to choose what they will write about. If the assignment is, say, a brief open response to a reading or a personal narrative, the unstructured assignment should pose no problems. But more complex writing tasks call for planning to overcome the problems I have been describing. Before students begin work, they should receive a description of the purpose of the assignment, its format, and the criteria that will be used in evaluating it. Students need to internalize and own the underlying purpose of the assignment so that they can select topics that will fulfill that purpose. Much class time has to be spent discussing topics and helping students define, limit, and focus what they expect to say. Class time alone is insufficient for many students, who will need individual attention during (and after) office hours. During the writing process, students should be required to submit plans, outlines, drafts, bibliographies, and other components because an open assignment makes it easy for them to omit parts of the complex task. Students should ask themselves at every stage, "Is this work fulfilling the original purpose of the assignment?" Meanwhile, both teacher and student must develop a common set of standards, and the teacher needs to know, by the frequent submissions, that the student is actually doing the work.

There is no doubt that this system helps some students write more effectively; it represents an ideal of teacher involvement with student writing that some institutions support for all assignments. But not often do we see this elaborate and labor-intensive pedagogy; few writing teachers have the time available. Open assignments more often reflect a lack of time than a commitment to intensive extra time with individual students. If you use open assignments, the job of developing individual topics is continuous.

Heuristic for the Writer of Writing Assignments

Erika Lindemann proposes a series of questions for faculty to ask themselves about their writing assignments; the following version of that heuristic (adapted from *A Rhetoric for Writing Teachers,* Oxford University Press, New York 1987. 196) exemplifies the kind of thinking that ought to go into the making of assignments that can support constructive writing instruction.

    A. Task Definition, Meaning, and Sequencing. What do I want the students to do? Is it worth doing? Why? Is it interesting and appropriate? What will it teach the students specifically? How does it fit my objectives at this point in the course? What can students do before they undertake the assignment, and where do I expect them to be after completing it? What will the assignment tell me? What is being assessed? Does the task have meaning outside as well as inside the class setting? Have I given enough class time to discussion of these goals?

    B. Writing Processes. How do I want the students to do the assignment? Are the students working alone or together? In what ways will they practice prewriting, writing, revising? Have I given enough information about what I want so that students can make effective choices about subject, purpose, form, mode, and tone? Have I given enough information about required length and about the use of sources? Have I prepared and distributed a written assignment with clear directions? Are good examples appropriate? Have I given enough class time to discussion of these procedures?

    C. Audience. For whom are the students writing? Who is the audience? If the audience is the teacher, do the students really know who the teacher is and what can be assumed? Are there ways and reasons to expand the audience beyond the teacher? Have I given enough class time to discussion of audience?

D. Schedule. When will students do the assignment? How does the assignment relate to what comes before and after it in the course? Is the assignment sequenced to give enough time for prewriting, writing, revision, and editing? How much time in and outside of class will students need? To what extent will I guide and grade the students' work? What deadlines (and penalties) do I want to set for collecting papers or for various stages of the project? Have I given enough class time to discussion of the writing process?

E. Assessment. What will I do with the assignment? How will I evaluate the work? What constitutes a successful response to the assignment? Will other students or the writer have a say in evaluating the paper? Does the grading system encourage revision? Have I attempted to write the paper myself? What problems did I encounter? How can the assignment be clarified or otherwise improved? Have I discussed evaluation criteria with the students before they began work, and will I discuss what I expect again as the due date approaches?

These guidelines for examining assignments must, of course, be adapted to the nature of the students, the curriculum, and the assignment. Not every question must be asked about typical short assignments or about in-class writing that is part of most writing classes, though many may apply. But the heuristic is particularly valuable for longer assignments. For example, the questions in point D relate directly to a deadline schedule for submission of stages of the work, if the writing is to be developed over a significant period of time. Depending on the assignment, this schedule could call for notes, bibliographies, abstracts, plans, outlines, sections, drafts, or whatever is most appropriate. A simple deadline schedule for each assignment has two important benefits: (1) It enforces the need for the student to get going quickly and to work steadily at the task, instead of trying to handle the assignment the night before the due date, and (2) it largely ensures that the work is the student's own, as early stages of a bought or borrowed paper are unlikely to be available.

Class Discussion of the Assignment

The written assignment must be discussed carefully with students. To illustrate just what the task calls for and how it will be assessed, I often hand out duplicated scoring guides (or develop one with the class) and samples of successful papers. Because few students will have experience meeting deadlines for plans or drafts, students will probably ignore them unless they are explained in detail. If enough time is allowed for discussion of the assignment, students will leave the class session with an understanding of what is required, why, and how to approach the job. They may even have developed some enthusiasm for the task, and they will know that a last-minute first draft will not be adequate. A properly discussed assignment reinforces the need to draft and revise drafts and distinguishes the cognitive work of revision from the editorial work of correcting errors. This last point is best made by distributing a former student's first draft (a good early draft, showing the discovery of the topic by the end), followed by that student's revision (rearranged so that the topic begins at the beginning and develops).

The construction of appropriate writing assignments is one of the hardest jobs for the teacher of undergraduates and is exacerbated by the dearth of supportive material available. Every teacher should keep in mind that designing assignments is a particularly demanding form of *writing*, calling for the teacher to use the entire writing process, most particularly revision with an eye to the audience. Careful consideration of the needs of the audience for the assignment and class discussion of the assignment, over the entire period when students are working on it, will help the teacher find out where students are having problems; reflection about these problems will often lead to a revised assignment for future classes.

Prewriting

Students will write better if they are required to think systematically before they put pen to paper. Although scholars debate what kinds of prewriting are most effective, there is a clear consensus that active engagement with an assignment before writing begins is immensely valuable; prewriting not only improves the quality of the work to be done but also trains students in a crucial part of the writing process. Some composition faculty use formal methods derived from logic or problem solving (sometimes called heuristics); other teachers use various forms of brainstorming, cognitive mapping, or clustering of ideas. Still others ask students to do unstructured five-minute writes, freewriting, or aptly named discovery drafts as ways to uncover or develop ideas. These are all forms of what classical rhetoric called *invention:* the finding of topics for development. The very word *topic* comes from the Greek word for "place," suggesting that the thinking process is a kind of geographic quest, a hunt for a place where ideas lurk.

Any assignment demanding substantial student effort is worth discussing in class as the work progresses. The most valuable discussion often emerges from presentation of what the other students in the class are working on. As students listen to their peers' plans, they begin to envision new possibilities. As they express their own thoughts on the subject, they begin to acquire ownership of their topic. Moreover, early notes and reading give them an unaccustomed start toward more satisfying writing than their previous training and habits may have led them to expect. Some teachers will break the class into small groups on the day that plans or outlines are due so that all students will be able to present their ideas to others in the class. The pressure of such a presentation is healthy; some students don't mind being unprepared for the teacher, but very few students are willing to look foolish before their peers.

SAMPLE ASSIGNMENTS FOR A WRITING COURSE

When we isolate writing assignments from the multitude of simultaneous tasks a teacher must accomplish, as this guide does, we focus attention on a major aspect of the writing course. Because the course revolves around student writing, not talking about student writing, the actual writing tasks are the center of action. Most student time should be spent writing to a planned sequence of topics; most teacher time should be spent responding to student writing. And most class time should be spent preparing for and responding to various stages in the writing process for that assignment. Thus it is appropriate to consider carefully each writing assignment and how it fits into the instructional plan for the course.

No set of writing assignments can lead to effective writing instruction without a clear plan for what each one should teach and an ordered sequence of instruction. The following assignments, however, offer support by giving many specific ways to plan thoroughly workable and interesting assignments. You will probably want to adapt them to your specific class before distributing them to your students, and you will need to develop an appropriate sequence of assignments for your own situation, but they have all been proved to work in composition classrooms. Some of the assignments are short classroom exercises; others are more elaborate. Some are designed as tests, others as papers to be revised and graded, and still others as material most useful for small group discussion with or without evaluation. In every case, the topic is followed by a few tips for scoring and for teaching. No writing assignment should ever be given without discussion of its expected purpose, audience, level of finish, and criteria for evaluation. If you give extended attention to these matters in class, you will get the best writing your students can produce, and you and they are likely to experience the satisfaction of achievement along with the inevitable frustration of writing.

Thus the assignments that follow are not set out as a curriculum to follow in a single course but rather as examples of assignments that might fit into an overall teaching plan. They move from simpler assignments, typically used in the early part of a course, to more complicated topics, appropriate for later on, but in no way have I attempted to design a single curriculum for all teachers and all students.

Understanding the Writing Process

Topic. Write a short paper in which you describe in detail your usual writing process. Then evaluate that process, giving its strengths and weaknesses.

Teaching and Scoring Tips. Class presentation of plans or drafts will let students see that everyone follows a writing process and that this process relates to individual styles of learning. Don't forget to describe your own writing process, too. When you describe criteria for assessing the paper, point out that you will reward vivid detail in the description of the writing process and clear connections between that detail and the evaluation of the student's own process. Weak papers will contain general descriptions and stock phrases ("I know I shouldn't write at the last minute, but that's life"). Remember that an unconventional and inappropriate writing process (for example, drafting the night before without revising) could still yield a good essay on this topic and that a good writing process does not guarantee a good essay.

Planning and Drafting

Understanding Writing Assignments

Topic. Define the possible meanings of the word *discuss* on a test. (Often that word follows a quotation.) To what extent does the word suggest such activities as defining, describing, comparing, contrasting, or evaluating? "Discuss" a test question that you have been given recently; state the question if you can remember it, and tell how you handled it.

Teaching and Scoring Tips. This is a difficult and abstract topic. Students who can't come up with an example may be lost; you might suggest using a dictionary to start with, or you might give a "*discuss*" question of your own for reference. Prewriting exercises (using the first word in the topic—for example, how does one "define" as part of an essay?) and some discussion in class are essential. Good students have usually learned the knack of redefining vague questions to fit what they know best while still responding to the question— a skill that other students need to learn. These latter students will learn it more effectively from listening to and discussing their peers' writing than from a lecture. The best essays will be able to draw clear distinctions among the options contained in the term *discuss* and will illustrate those distinctions with some detail.

Thinking of Your Audience

Topic. Think of the last really good cultural, social, or sports event you attended, and describe it in three different ways: first to your best friend, then to your parents, and then to a group of high school students attending an open house at your college. Finally, describe the variations in content, organization, and wording that writing for different audiences led you to make.

Teaching and Scoring Tips. This is a four-part assignment, the last part of which calls for examination of the first three, according to three categories. (That really makes it a six-part or even a nine-part assignment.) Be sure to make clear just what you really want because the assignment looks simpler than it is. If you want all nine parts, give the students enough space and time to do them; if you want less, make clear what an acceptable response will include. This is a good topic for peer evaluation in small groups, where the audience is visible.

Exploring a Topic

Topic. Describe how you would proceed to write a paper on the following topic: "White-collar crime poses a greater danger to the economy than more visible forms of street crime." Include (1) a list of actions you would take to gather information and define your terms and (2) an outline or other plan for presenting your ideas. In your presentation, make clear that you see the difference between *asserting* ideas and *demonstrating* ideas.

Teaching and Scoring Tips. Help students see that this is a topic about planning a paper—a brand-new concept for many. The best papers will show awareness of the complexity of definition, familiarity with the use of sources, and some sense of the process of demonstrating ideas. Weak papers will slide into clichés about crime (instead of focusing on the topic) and may use an outline format without real reference to the problems at hand. If the plans look promising, you might ask students to go ahead and write the paper. They should keep notes in writing logs or journals (if you have your students keep them) about changes in the plan as their process proceeds.

Revising and Editing

Topic. Select a paper of more than two pages in length that you have written for this course. In preparation for revision, number each paragraph, and write a single complete sentence that states what each paragraph is saying. (If a paragraph is saying more than one thing, without a unifying connection, it probably needs to be divided into two or more paragraphs.) Examine your list of sentences, and write a response to each of the following questions:

1. How have you organized the main ideas of your paper? spatially? chronologically? logically? Or do they occur at random? Is the organization effective?

2. Do all the ideas relate to a central idea and to one another?

3. Can you identify any confusing leaps from point to point?

4. Looking at the sentences *and* your paper, can you identify transitions—words or phrases that connect ideas? Do any others need to be added?

5. Have any points been left out?

6. Are any included points irrelevant?

7. Where is the best, most original, most interesting, most important idea located? If it comes late in the paper, as it often does in early drafts, write a new outline putting that idea up front, in a prominent place. Then rearrange the other paragraphs as needed.

8. What are the strengths and weaknesses of your original organization? How might the organization of the paper be improved?

Hand in (1) the original paper, (2) your numbered series of sentences outlining the paragraph structure, and (3) your responses to the eight questions, including the new outline, if needed.

Teaching and Scoring Tips. Most students are reluctant to go back to a paper they have "finished" and rework it, so class time will be necessary to help them understand the importance of revising and reading their own writing critically. Some students have acquired the romantic belief that writing is the result of inspiration and that revision is a betrayal of the muse. (It is a major irony that the most professional writers revise all the time, whereas the least skilled writers almost never do.) And many students have no experience reading their own writing critically. For many, this will be the first time they have ever had seriously to rethink, revise (which literally means "see anew"), or rewrite (as opposed to edit) a paper. A successful response to this assignment will show that the student has been able to see the original paper anew and to move beyond editing to reorganizing it; the exercise is designed to free the student from the limits of the early draft, which to inexperienced writers often seems so fixed that nothing can be dropped or added or shifted about.

Constructing and Analyzing Argument

Topic. Create a complete argumentative thesis statement for two of the following general topics:

1. The Arab-Israeli Conflict

2. Mandatory testing of prison inmates for HIV

3. Acquaintance rape

4. A new federal student-loan program

5. A college ban on fraternities and sororities

Teaching and Scoring Tips. Note that the thesis statement should specify the following components: purpose, audience, definite position, and reasons why the position is true. In essence, the thesis will state, "In this essay, I plan to [explain, argue, demonstrate, illustrate] for an audience of ____ that _____ because _____." This appears to be a dry formula, but students will give it life as they apply it to real arguments and relate it to their own experience; meanwhile, its very rigidity requires that they consider the crucial issues for a thesis statement. You will want to help students understand the difference between arguable and nonarguable statements and between asserting and demonstrating ideas. The thesis statements (really opening paragraphs) written on this topic are particularly useful for small group discussion; the groups could give one point for each of the components required and two points for an arguable assertion. Though you may not want to ask students to complete the essays for which they have written thesis statements, you might want to discuss with them ways of developing the planned arguments—in particular, what sources might be used, what tone might be most effective, and what sequence of arguments might be most convincing. The creation of thesis statements also helps students make an informed choice among topics; the most complete, best-argued thesis statement will not only identify the topic on which they are likely to be most successful but also the most interesting one. (This procedure will help students perform well on the many essay tests that give a choice of topic.)

Constructing Paragraphs

Constructing Unified, Coherent, and Well-developed Paragraphs

Topic. Select a well-developed paragraph from an essay you have written recently. At the top of a sheet of paper, copy that paragraph. Below it, write another paragraph showing why the paragraph you selected is a good one: Identify its central idea (usually embodied in a topic sentence), show how each sentence relates to the central idea, and describe the pattern of development (illustration, definition, comparison/contrast, and so on). If you see ways in which the paragraph might have been improved, go ahead and rewrite it.

Teaching and Scoring Tips. Even weak students know more about paragraphing than they are consciously aware of. But conscious awareness of paragraphing often extends no further than the notion of indenting the first line. This exercise asks students to use what they are learning about paragraphs as part of their own revision process. Because many students have great difficulty reading what they have written (clouded by what they perhaps meant to say), small group discussion of this exercise should compare the paragraph analysis of the author to that of others in the group.

Developing Main Ideas

Topic. Choose one of the topic sentences that follow, and write a unified paragraph that develops the main ideas.

1. I found out quickly that college life was not quite what I had expected.

2. Being part of the in crowd used to be of prime importance to me.

3. My work experience has taught me several important lessons.

4. Until recently, I never appreciated my parents fully.

5. I expect my college education to do more than simply ensure me a job.

Teaching and Scoring Tips. The best paragraphs will (1) supply details and other evidence, (2) use a clear organizational plan, (3) employ cohesive and transitional devices, and (4) develop the idea sufficiently to suggest a convincing argument. Each of these four aspects of developed paragraphs is worth discussion when the assignment is given, and each of them should be attended to when you (or peer groups) respond to and evaluate the paragraphs produced. One prewriting exercise would be to select one of the topic sentences (or to come up with a similar one) for the class to develop on the chalkboard. Write out the proposed sentence, and act as scribe as students propose sentences to follow; revise steadily, with an eye to the four issues you expect to evaluate in a finished paragraph. How good is the paragraph you come up with? If you wanted to take more time and effort, how might it be improved further? Keep asking yourself how well you have modeled a revision process.

Constructing Grammatical Sentences

Topic. The following sentences contain unnecessary words and phrases. Rewrite them so that they are clear and concise.

1. At the present time, many different forms of hazing occur, such as various forms of physical abuse and also mental abuse.

2. Many people have a tendency toward the expansion of their sentences by the superfluous addition of extra words that are not really needed for the meaning of the sentences.

3. One of the major problems that is faced at this point in time is that there is world hunger.

4. After I stopped the practice of exercising regularly, I put on ten pounds of weight in a relatively short amount of time.

5. There are numerous theories that have been proposed by scientists as to why dinosaurs reached the point of becoming extinct.

Teaching and Scoring Tips. Improving the bad sentences that other people write is good fun and not very difficult, even for students who have a hard time producing good sentences of their own. Take enough class time with this set of sentences to discuss both the problems and the alternative improvements that the students will suggest. (Do not imply that there is only one correct answer for any sentence.) The problem in teaching this kind of useful exercise is to achieve some transfer of practice from the exercise to the students' prose. Much research has shown that the ability to see or correct errors in other people's writing does not lead a person directly to being a better writer; one's own sentences are designed to carry meaning for a purpose and an audience, not merely to be correct. Nonetheless, knowledge about ways to improve writing can provide a context for improvement when student writing is carefully annotated for a particular trait. This exercise will not by itself lead to the production of improved sentences by your students. But exercises like this are worth doing if you make them meaningful by connecting such work to actual sentences to be revised in the students' own writing.

Hence, you must make explicit connections between this set of sentences and student work. One way to do this would be to follow the exercise with small group reading of draft paragraphs from work in progress. Each student should seek sentences that need improvement in the paragraphs before the group. But in every case, the group will have to be sensitive to the purpose and audience of the work in question and not merely simplify for the sake of simplifying; it is easy to simplify sentences out of context but far more difficult to do so with attention to the complex meanings and emotions of real writing.

Another way to make connections is for you to relate one or two sentences in student work to sentences in the exercises: "This sentence," you might write in the margin, "has some characteristics of sentence 5 in our last exercise. Try to improve it along the lines of our revision of that sentence in class."

Using Dictionaries

Topic. Look up the word *sophistication* in several dictionaries, and write an essay in which you explain the meanings the word may have in various contexts. In your essay, consider the Greek root and the complex history of the word.

Teaching and Scoring Tips. This topic is interesting because of its complexity; most students think it a compliment to be called a "sophisticated" person, but wine connoisseurs are appalled at "sophisticated" wine. Buried inside the word are the contradictory attitudes we tend to feel about wisdom and ignorance (or innocence). Intelligent use of the dictionary leads to awareness of this complexity, not, as some "unsophisticated" students believe, to simple answers. Students at a stage of development where they expect things to be either right or wrong or expect authorities (such as the dictionary) to settle problems will have a hard time with this essay. They will need some help coping with ambiguity and with approaching the dictionary as a start rather than an end of questions about words.

Varying Register

Topic. Write five sentences about one of the subjects listed here in which you use the familiar register, as if you were writing or talking to a very close friend. Then work those sentences through the necessary changes to make them first informal and then formal. You should have produced fifteen sentences. Finally, write a short essay of three or four paragraphs on the problems you encountered as you tried to move from register to register.

1. New friends versus old friends

2. The difficulty of getting homework done

3. Balancing schoolwork and a job

4. Gaining or losing weight

Teaching and Scoring Tips. This is an almost impossible task for inexperienced writers, so it should be treated as a learning exercise not to be graded. You may have to devote class time to explaining and defining register, or you may refer students to that section in their handbooks. Many students, when they arrive at college, will have many registers for speech but only one register for writing, a dead formal tone they have grown accustomed to using in school. Such a tone is often rewarded by high grades, praised as "objective," even required in some disciplines. This exercise is intended to free students from these restraints, loosen them up, help them find new possibilities, and move toward a more genuine voice. One way to help students see the many options they have is to begin with the many oral registers they use with their families, friends, and social groups. You may wish to substitute topics more suited to your particular group of students, as long as the topics elicit genuine sentences for a variety of audiences.

Analyzing Experience

Topic. Describe and analyze an institution or a group of some sort that you knew well as a child: A school, school group, scout troop, dancing class, summer camp, club, Sunday school—any group with an internally consistent set of unambiguous values you can see clearly will serve. You have two specific jobs to accomplish: to describe clearly what it was like to be a member of the group at the time and to assess from your mature perspective the meaning of the group's values.

Teaching and Scoring Tips. This assignment draws on descriptive personal writing and adds to it a demand for analysis. The first task here is to help students select an institution to describe and analyze. Because almost any group can meet the demands of the assignment, they have many possible choices. As part of the job will be to see the institution from two different time perspectives (past and present), it should be a group that they remember well enough to describe clearly but from which they have some distance.

The first essay test topic in Chapter 3 (p. 50) of this guide is excellent preparation for this assignment, and the sample student papers in that chapter can lead to useful class discussion. Note that the essay test topic, designed for forty-five minutes of writing time, is simpler in its demands than this essay. You might want to bring in some examples of professional writing on this topic such as Paul Fussell's *The Boy Scout Handbook* (1982).

Suggestions from you and from students in the class will make the possibilities clear. Perhaps, you might suggest, a summer camp loved (or hated) as a child would be fun to revisit in writing, but it may be just as rosy (or bleak) in memory today as it was in the past; maybe there isn't much to say about it beyond description. But as students reflect on, say, the high school band, some questions arise that would be interesting to pursue: Maybe some student loved music when she joined but learned to dislike music because of the intense competition inside the group; that is a topic rich with possibilities. Or perhaps a scout troop changed the way someone thinks and feels even today: How did the group do that? Perhaps as students think about the values of the groups they remember, they may find some conflict between what was said and what was done; such inconsistencies are always interesting to examine.

Early drafts are likely to be mostly description, for analyzing values is a difficult task that usually requires both distance and insight; good description, particularly if it handles the two locations in time clearly, surely deserves praise and reward. But a revision should move beyond description into analysis of meaning. Because the topic is inherently interesting to students, they will often be able to come up with creative insights into what was really going on in their pasts.

Expect a wide variety in students' ability to examine their pasts, a skill that depends on the development of metacognitive skills and maturity. For instance, some students will be able to look at a church school designed to keep them from asking questions about religion with amusement and insight; other students will be defensive and protective about their childhood religions. Again, some students will be able to analyze the competitive aspects of American education (such as spelling bees) as evidence of a competitive society, while others may be so committed to competition as a value that they see in those phenomena only reason and good sense. Some students may even feel that to question the institutions they knew as children is subversive (which in fact it is) and un-American (which it is not). One good way to help unsophisticated students develop the needed analytic skills is to form small groups for discussion of possible topics after class discussion; students will learn well from each other and be less defensive than they will in the class as a whole.

A sample response to this assignment, in two drafts, along with commentary by the teacher on the drafts and in conference, appears in Chapter 6 of this book.

Becoming a Researcher

Topic. Write a short essay examining what the anthropologist Jules Henry means in the following passage and showing the extent to which the passage applies to your own schooling.

Another learning problem inherent in the human condition is the fact that we must conserve culture while changing it; that we must always be *more* sure of surviving than of adapting—*as we see it.* Whenever a new idea appears, our first concern as *animals* must be that it does not kill us; then and only then can we look at it from other points of view. In general, primitive people solved this problem simply by walling their children off from new possibilities by educational methods that, largely by fear (including ridicule, beating and mutilation), so narrowed the perceptual sphere that other than traditional ways of viewing the world became unthinkable. . . . The function of education has never been to free the mind and the spirit of man, but to bind them. . . . Schools have therefore never been places for the stimulation of young minds.
   —From Jules Henry, *Culture against Man*, New York: Random House, 1963. 286–88

Teaching and Scoring Tips. The basic problem in teaching the research paper is to reverse students' preconception that research means collecting other people's opinions and patching them together with a bit of rhetorical glue. Thus it is a good idea to begin with an analytical reading of a single source such as this one to demonstrate ways of using a source as part of one's own paper. This passage is particularly good for such a purpose because many conventional students have a hard time understanding that a respectable person would say such a radical thing about the schools they have been told to love; other students may find that Henry is saying what they have often felt but never quite dared to say. So students must begin by understanding the meaning of what the writer has to say (through class discussion of the passage and its context) and how that meaning relates to what they have to say about their own schooling. Then they must integrate what Henry says into their papers.

   The students' abilities should determine how much class time to give to prewriting. If the class is very able, you might wait for submission of first drafts before discussing the passage, even though many of the students will misunderstand what Henry says and will write essays defending school spirit. Well-trained students enjoy the challenge of discovering a new idea on their own and will come to class primed for discussion. Numbers of good students may misread the passage as an attack on American schools instead of a statement about the function of all schools. Resist discussion of bad examples of student writing, which do not teach as well as good ones. Some of the drafts will be good enough to illustrate for the rest of the class the way to respond to a quotation that seems to attack values one treasures. The writers of these papers will understand and discuss the Henry passage, refer to it in proper form, and bring some experiences from their own schooling to demonstrate the degree to which the passage helps them understand those experiences.

A weaker class will need more help, though, ironically, it may be more ready to deal with what Henry says about schools. Put *Culture Against Man* on reserve in the library, or find a legal way to photocopy the chapter and ask such a class to read the chapter from which the passage comes and to write a summary of its argument. Help students understand some of the ways in which anthropologists observe cultures; Henry is applying these techniques to our own culture rather than one in a far-off land. When the summaries are brought in, you might well analyze the chapter with the class and construct on the chalkboard an outline of the principal assertions in the chapter. A lively discussion of school experiences will surely follow, leading to many ideas about ways to handle the topic assigned. Several drafts may be necessary before the students have learned how to refer to a source in the course of developing their own essays. But until they have reached that point, it is of no value to assign a research paper.

Assigning a Research Paper

Why Require a Research Paper?

The research paper has been slipping out of fashion in recent years. Many educators see it as a product- and footnote-oriented exercise with little meaning. They will argue that research depends on a background of knowledge that first-year students do not have, so students wind up going through the motions of research without assimilating its substance. Besides, the argument goes, different disciplines have different ways of doing and writing about research, reflecting unique discourse communities; teaching research techniques must therefore be the job of a student's major. Some writing teachers enlist the aid of faculty in the various disciplines to support discussion of discourse communities; more advanced courses might even require students to choose a field or even a professional journal as their audience.

The advantages of requiring a research paper in beginning college writing courses remain clear, however, despite the power of these arguments for specialization. All first-year students need to learn how to incorporate source material into their own writing, and that task cannot wait for advanced courses in the major, which are likely to assume that students have already learned general research skills. Evidence from research is not much different from other kinds of evidence that students must learn to use in papers to demonstrate ideas, and hence freshman composition can, or even should, teach this aspect of exposition.

It is certainly possible to assign a research paper and to teach the use of research materials in the writing course without resorting to empty forms and formats. If you decide to use a research paper, you might want to restrict the number of sources and the extent of the paper, and you will probably want to emphasize the various stages of the paper at least as much as the final product. Above all, you will want to emphasize that research uses sources to answer interesting questions, not to impress with their quantity, length, or style. Any quotation inserted into a paper must be discussed and connected to the controlling idea; quotations can support ideas but may never substitute for them.

The research paper can remain in the writing class, if it loses its curse as a dead exercise in compiling quotations in correct form. It has an appropriate place as an important kind of writing, with its own process issues and its own problems with evidence. Indeed, some teachers will design the entire writing course as a sequence of assignments (including ones that I suggest in this chapter) linked to the writing of the research paper, which might incorporate earlier assignments. This is one way to give coherence and continuity to the sequence of writing assignments, though not, of course, the only way.

Selecting Topics

Many teachers are reluctant to prescribe topics for research because they believe that research depends on the writer's individual curiosity about a subject. Such a view makes sense as long as the development of a clear and manageable topic becomes the joint responsibility of the student and the teacher, with early decisions about a topic required. Inexperienced writers will confuse identification of an area of inquiry with selection of a writing topic, and they normally need help in seeing the difference. An area of inquiry is usually too large to manage: "What is the meaning of love in poetry?" A writing topic focuses and narrows that area of interest and poses a question that can be addressed in the time and space allowed: "Sexual love versus spiritual love in the poetry of John Donne." For students with sufficient ability and teachers with sufficient time, the selection of a topic might well be part of the writing task and the writing process. But other faculty, faced with this problem of clear topic definition but with insufficient time to spend with each student (or, perhaps, concerned about the ready availability of commercial research papers), will prefer to assign a particular area of inquiry for their students. The students' freedom of choice becomes restricted, but the advantages of precision, focus, and economy of time may well compensate.

Sample Topic

The following topic is an example of a research paper assignment that narrows focus for the student sharply but also allows considerable choice.

Topic. The term *popular art* is loosely used to describe the kind of literature, music, painting, architecture, and other cultural matter that is produced for unsophisticated mass consumption. Some popular art sometimes turns out to be very sophisticated indeed (Dickens's novels, for instance), but most popular art is designed to reaffirm and comfort popular attitudes and tastes, not challenge or examine them.

Choose for this paper a relatively unsophisticated form of popular art for analysis. If you choose a type, or genre, be sure that it is a coherent genre—not "popular music" but, say, "sentimental love songs of the 1950s," not "comic books" but "Disney comics" or "monster comics" or "superhero-type comics." Popular art exists in almost all areas, for all kinds of specialized interests. Be sure to select a form of popular art in a field you find interesting to begin with.

Your object will be to have something worth saying about the material you analyze and then to express what you have to say convincingly. Evidence for your argument will probably come for the most part from analysis or descriptions of the popular art. But one requirement of the paper is that you consult relevant material about popular art and find a way to make use of at least three different sources on your subject in your paper. An incidental but required job is for you to learn and use standard ways of referring to these sources.

Teaching and Scoring Tips. This assignment has several strengths as a research paper topic. It combines considerable focus with openness of choice for the student. That is, students can write about a wide variety of material, from comic books to tract homes, from horror movies to bumper stickers, from Nancy Drew to Neil Simon, but they have already been given a substantial head start on ways to approach the material. Similarly, the range of sources has been limited, and attention is placed on the development of ideas rather than on the accumulation of note cards. Class time should be spent discussing topics (perhaps giving each student a few minutes to present ideas for consideration), sources (students should know about the *Journal of Popular Culture*, for instance), and ways of using sources to develop ideas. It is advisable to specify at least three deadlines: (1) an early one, requiring a thesis statement of the main idea and an annotated bibliography; (2) an intermediate one, requiring a completed draft for peer group evaluation of ideas, organization, and use of sources; and (3) a final deadline for the edited draft, with a high level of polish. Most students will need yet another chance to revise that final draft before the product is satisfactory.

SELECTED REFERENCES

Ruth, Leo, and Sandra Murphy. *Designing Writing Tasks for the Assessment of Writing.* Norwood, NJ: Ablex, 1988.
White, Edward M. "Assessment and the Design of Effective Writing Assignments." *Teaching and Assessing Writing: Recent Advances in Understanding, Evaluating, and Improving Student Performance.* 2nd ed. San Francisco: Jossey-Bass, 1994. 21–51.

CHAPTER 2

HELPING STUDENTS DO WELL ON ESSAY TESTS

<=>

ESSAY TESTS AND WRITING ASSESSMENT

Twenty years ago, the timed impromptu essay test was everywhere defended by English faculty as the most effective, responsible, and teacher-supportive assessment device available—a humanistic response to the machinery of multiple-choice tests. But essay testing has been under attack recently in the professional literature for requiring first-draft writing to a set topic under artificial, tension-producing circumstances; though essay testing remains standard practice, educators emphasizing the writing process and the importance of revision are often suspicious of the results of an assessment device that now seems distant from their teaching. For such instructors, the assessment tool of choice is likely to be portfolios, which can include a wider range of writing and writing processes.

But portfolios have their own problems and may not be a practical alternative (see Chapter 7). A 1992 unpublished survey by a committee of the Conference on College Composition shows that over 70 percent of colleges and universities that assess writing use some form of impromptu essay as part of

25

their writing assessments; clearly, the essay test has gained credibility as a direct measure of writing ability and has made important inroads against the prevailing tendency to use multiple-choice tests for that purpose. Even proponents of writing as a process can argue that evaluation of an achieved writing product is appropriate, for the only way to come up with the product is through some sort of process. Essay tests have important strengths as well as limitations, and we ought not to exaggerate either.

The limitations of the impromptu essay test have become clear as portfolios have become prominent, in that portfolios are a kind of expanded essay test, covering much time, allowing for revision, including several topics. Here are the most important limitations of essay tests:

- The essay test defines writing as first-draft writing, thereby contradicting the definition of writing as a process.

- The essay test yields a score on a one-question test, which may disadvantage a student who cannot do well with that particular question.

- The essay test is an artificial exercise, under anxiety-producing test conditions, requiring writing to a set topic, and hence may not represent more natural writing circumstances.

- Essay test scores are often misused, as if they reflected students' true writing ability rather than their responses to a particular question on a test under time constraints.

We must recognize the existence of these limitations, even if we note that the strengths of essay testing may compensate for them. Here are some of the strengths of essay tests:

- Essay tests are much preferable to multiple-choice tests because writing requires students to generate ideas, sentences, and conclusions rather than merely react passively to given choices.

- The intense concentration required by an essay test can lead to representative writing that correlates well with the way students write under less pressured conditions.

- A well-designed essay test allows students to demonstrate their writing process.

- Essay test scores are no more likely to be misused than other assessment results, but if they are scored responsibly by the writing staff, they can support the teaching of writing.

• An essay written under test conditions is indisputably the product of the student being assessed. And test conditions are not necessarily improper, considering that all school writing is artificial and all writing induces a certain amount of anxiety in most students.

• Using focused holistic scoring, we can grade an essay test rapidly and reliably. (For a detailed description of the process, see Edward M. White, *Teaching and Assessing Writing*, 2nd ed., San Francisco: Jossey-Bass, 1994. Chap. 10.)

In light of these arguments, many institutions will continue to ask writing teachers to develop, supervise, and score essay tests. And instructors in all disciplines will see such tests as a reasonable way to assess student writing for in-class as well as institutional purposes. Hence, writing teachers should continue to take seriously their opportunity to help students do well on essay tests, which will recur throughout the college years.

Some students do very well on essay tests. If they have learned how to read essay questions (which often means mentally revising the questions into clearer and more manageable ones), if they have experience at organizing their thoughts quickly, if they have ready fluency in the school dialect (without oral dialect or foreign language interference), and if they have quick editing skills, they are likely to succeed. One sign of privilege in our society, in fact, is the early ability to demonstrate these skills, which are the province of the private preparatory schools and a few of the best high schools. Not that these schools spend much time teaching test-taking skills. The students often pick them up from each other, as a kind of lore, based on self-confidence and expectations of success.

But many students have never learned those skills and consequently do much worse than they should on essay tests. Many students from weak educational systems have done very little writing, and the little they have done has been more or less the mechanical repetition of information. For most students, writing means retelling something that they have read or that the teacher has said, and such impersonal and unorganized writing may have been rewarded with praise and high grades, particularly outside of English courses. Suddenly, in college, these students are confronted with essay tests that call for original thought, organization, and editing, all within a tight time limit. Moreover, for a significant number, the dialect required is a great distance from that spoken everywhere but at school. Little wonder that essay tests provoke fear and hostility in these students!

We will be doing our students a great service if we spend some time helping them learn the test-taking skills that the privileged absorb along with their advanced placement courses. Even those who have picked up these skills will benefit from understanding what they have been doing and how they might do it even better. This chapter is designed to help teachers find ways to do this.

UNDERSTANDING THE QUESTION

Two problems cloud the understanding of essay questions: Teachers often do not make clear what is called for, and even when they do, students do not attend carefully to the demands of the question.

Writing Clear Essay Questions

Well-constructed essay questions often use a series of code words that students must understand: *describe, discuss, compare, contrast, explain, comment,* and others with even less obvious meanings. Some handbooks and manuals define these terms, making clear distinctions among them (for example, see section 49b in *The St. Martin's Handbook*). Unfortunately, teachers spend little time reading these handbooks, so students must expect considerable overlap and ambiguity, even when the words seem distinct. The problem is not that teachers or students do not understand what the terms mean; the fact is that the terms have no fixed meaning and can mean whatever the teacher expects them to mean.

For example, many teachers will use *compare* as a direction to show similarities between two objects or views and *contrast* as a direction to show differences; most handbooks define the terms in this way. Thus "compare and contrast" will often mean to do both: describe similarities and differences. But other teachers (and handbooks) will take *compare* to include *contrast*, on the logical grounds that comparing two things means placing them side by side and describing what matters. A diligent student who has learned the narrower definition of *compare* and cites only similarities in such a case will receive half credit; a protest that the teacher should have asked specifically for contrasts if differences were to be shown is likely to fall on deaf ears.

Because of the uncertainty of these terms, careful question design is likely to avoid them or explain them, for clarity's sake. The best way to explain them is probably to take class time to define and illustrate the meaning of test terms for a particular class, perhaps referring students to this section in the handbook you assign or keep in a writing lab. An awkward substitute would be to define the terms on the test itself. Another useful way to proceed is to create questions with explicit instructions. Thus instead of directing students to "compare and contrast" two quotations, a question could ask students to "show in what ways these two quotations are saying similar things and in what ways they are saying different things." The longer version is somewhat cumbersome, but it does not depend on students' knowing the ill-defined meanings of *compare* and *contrast*. But, of course, a student would have to know what *show* means (does it include "use specific detail"?) in order to proceed, so there is no way to avoid using some sort of code.

An even more common example of a confusing direction is the overused term *discuss*. Many teachers will use this directive when they mean something as vague as "say something about the subject." For many students, this turns out to be an activity analogous to what in computer talk is called a "file dump": an undifferentiated list of all information available, without organization, coherence, or context. A high grade can be earned for such a file dump—if that was the teacher's intent. But the teacher may well mean—indeed, ought to mean—something much more precise, such as an argument about the strengths and weaknesses of a particular position. In that case, the file dump will elicit a low grade and complaints about inability to focus and organize. In fact, the teacher has received what was asked for but not what was really sought. The miscommunication that results from imprecise question design leads students into confusion and teachers into frustration.

Students will benefit from practice-reading essay questions with pen in hand. In the first place, they should recognize and circle the key directions and consider what the words mean. Many students interpret all directive words as "say something about" (which is in fact all that many teachers mean) and need to understand that different directions may actually call for different kinds of responses. They should be aware that *describe* usually requires specific detail, that *explain* is likely to call for definitions and analysis, that *analyze* suggests taking something apart to see what it is made of, and so on. Here are some other terms that teachers use in question design, along with what they often mean by them:

List Name one by one, explaining or commenting when appropriate

Enumerate List in a meaningful sequence

Outline Give an overall plan for proceeding in some kind of order

Design Present a more elaborate overall plan than an outline, using descriptions, sketches, drawings, or the like

Summarize State the main points in as concise a way as possible, without commentary

Review Give a quick survey of several positions, using summaries with commentary

Interpret Explain in detail what something means to you and how you came to that understanding

Define Present in detail the essential traits or characteristics of something and how it differs from similar things

Prove Provide evidence to establish that something is true

Demonstrate Add to your proof examples of applications of what you have shown to be true

I have not listed *discuss* because I cannot come up with a definition of the term that distinguishes it from "say something about." I have also not tried to make the list complete. But two conclusions from this brief look at examination terminology are unavoidable: Teachers who have a clear sense of what they want their students to do on a writing assignment need to use directions beyond the confusing code words, and teachers who do not have a clear sense of the task they are requiring should understand (and perhaps attempt to complete) their own assignments before they ask their students to do so.

Further, students should be taught to note and circle the different *parts* of the question. A common cause of low grades on essays is simply failing to answer all parts of the question. It is easy to get caught up in responding to the first directive and to forget everything else. If students circle and number the parts (which may be buried in a complex sentence), they are more likely to deal with them. Even advanced students will often miss key parts of complex questions. One question type asks for a single coherent essay in which several topics are addressed. Many students will answer the subquestions in a series of paragraphs, sometimes numbering them diligently, but fail to connect these parts into the single coherent essay required.

Finally, students need to be aware of the mode of discourse that the question requires. This can be a serious problem for first-year students, who often have little experience with expository writing. We seem, at the close of the twentieth century in America, to have reversed the findings of James Britton and his team of researchers in the London schools some decades ago. They found very little personal writing and a great deal of rote expository writing. Today many of our students have very little practice with expository writing; personal narratives are all they can produce. It is now common to find personal essays as responses on college placement tests, even when the question specifically asks for exposition or argument. One sure way for a student to fail an institutionally administered expository essay question is to answer it with a personal experience.

Some questions may intentionally mix modes: "Analyze the quotation and then illustrate it by some personal experience." Students need to see that such a question expects the narrative to be subordinate to the discussion of the quotation and connected to it. Sometimes the emphasis seems to be reversed: "Describe an occasion in which you _____, and tell what you learned from it." This question normally elicits a personal narrative with a perfunctory moral tag on the end. Perhaps such a narrative and tag are what the question actually seeks, but often what is really required is very much like the analysis in the preceding question. If there are good reasons to believe that the question is in fact basically looking for exposition, the student should decide on the concept first and use the description to illustrate the concept, writing an expository paper, with its evidence drawn from personal experience, not a personal narrative.

Sometimes, particularly on short placement tests, a narrative or a description is all that the question calls for. Though not all students find personal or descriptive writing easier than expository writing, most do; such writing poses few organizational or interpretive problems, for a simple chronology will usually serve quite well and the student is the final expert on the meaning of his or her own experiences. Such a test will examine a student's ability to marshal memories in reasonably error-free Standard English.

The point is to train students to read questions carefully and to gain sufficient experience at writing in different modes so that they can make a rapid, accurate judgment of the kind of writing that may be required on an essay test. As more and more instructors are learning to ask precise questions, students are more and more likely to encounter clear directives. They may not know why the clear test strikes them as a good one or why they feel more capable and successful as they answer it, but they will be pleased with teaching and testing that clarifies rather than confuses.

Responding to Unclear Essay Questions

Unfortunately, many essay questions are not designed with sufficient care or precision, and students have come to expect vague questions on essay tests. Even well-trained and experienced students may be surprised to receive low grades on a precise essay question because they have not responded to the question asked; some students are so used to unclear questions that they have become accustomed to ignoring them and writing whatever they choose on the general topic. Writing teachers must prepare students for the unclear questions they will be asked in various courses and must help students differentiate among types of unclear questions. Most of all, students need to know when a question makes precise demands that they must follow and when it requires them to construct their own question.

When a question is not clear, it becomes the student's responsibility to construct a clear question and then answer it. This way of handling the question is never evident, and many students will respond to unclear questions as they do to the ubiquitous *discuss*, by simply dumping everything they know about the topic on the page in the hope that they will somehow hit on whatever the teacher is looking for. Sometimes that works, for a vague question suggests that the teacher has no clear response in mind. But a much more productive tactic for students is to figure out what a reasonable question might be in relation to what is asked and to the context of the test.

For example, on the final exam in a course dealing with nineteenth-century European symphonies, the class finds the following question: "Beethoven and Brahms. 30 minutes." Many possibilities open up. Some students in the class begin writing immediately, telling everything they know about Beethoven (mostly his biography, with dates of the symphonies), followed by whatever they can list about Brahms, with dates; at the end, when time is up, they stop in midsentence and scrawl, "Out of time."

More experienced test-taking students do not start writing without revising and clarifying the question. They take five of the thirty minutes to list on scratch paper a few connections between the two composers, recognizing that the question must represent some kind of comparison and contrast. They know that they can write only three or so paragraphs, so they decide that one paragraph will deal with similarities and a second with differences; a final paragraph will address the importance of the two composers in the history of music; an opening paragraph is uncertain, so they leave space for it to be added at the end of the test, stating the question that they have answered. These successful students might produce an opening paragraph stating that Beethoven and Brahms are both German Romantic composers who displayed different forms of romanticism; two paragraphs might follow, comparing and contrasting a few aspects of their romanticism; and a closing paragraph could suggest that later composers such as Bruckner and Mahler drew on both forms of romanticism. Writing ends with a few minutes to spare, so they reread their essays, fix up the spelling, insert a missing word or two, and move on to the next question.

The excellent students I have just described may or may not happen to know more about nineteenth-century music than the mediocre students, writing as fast as they can without a plan, but they will certainly get higher grades. They will also find essay tests more rewarding and less exasperating than the other students will.

Sometimes the questions are even less clear than "Beethoven and Brahms." A typical one will give a quotation with no directive at all, or the quotation may be followed by the direction "Discuss." But what is the student to discuss? Again, most students will proceed with a file dump, disgorging as much of what they know as possible on the page. But the careful, well-trained student will pause to construct a question before responding so that the essay can follow some kind of organization. What is the quotation saying, and how does it relate to the material of the course? (Most essays written in response to texts fail to examine the text in much detail.)

These students will mark up the quotation and sketch out meanings and connections as they decide on the central idea of their response. If time is short, they may begin by leaving space for an opening paragraph and proceed to write an analysis paragraph, expecting their own point to become clear as they write. Soon they realize that the quotation illustrates a particular point of view, perhaps a common mistake or a particular insight, in the field; the task then becomes to show how the quotation achieves its goal: an analysis question. Or perhaps the quotation needs to be proved, or disproved, by an ordered citation of evidence: The question calls for an argument. Whatever the students decide, it is impossible for them to write out an answer until they have a good sense of even a badly written question.

For example, consider the first question in Chapter 4 of this book, a question based on a Samuel Clemens quotation:

The best swordsman in the world doesn't need to fear the second best swordsman in the world; no, the person for him to be afraid of is some ignorant antagonist who has never had a sword in his hand before; he doesn't do the thing he ought to do, and so the expert isn't prepared for him; he does the thing he ought not to do; and often it catches the expert out and ends him on the spot.

An early draft of this question used the quotation with only a vague directive, and many students had a great deal of trouble with it. Some were convinced that they should devote themselves to a discussion of dueling; others decided to call up whatever they knew about Clemens and so relate the quotation to *Tom Sawyer* and *Huckleberry Finn*. Many students began writing about dueling as an example of something, only gradually coming to realize the essence of the quotation; by then it was too late to revise and reorganize the essay. The most astute and test-wise students marked up the quotation carefully, usually by underlining the three characters whose actions are being described: the best swordsman, the second best swordsman, and the ignorant antagonist. These students listed descriptors and examples for the three character types. A typical example looked like this:

Best swordsman: expert, like the Redcoats in 1776

Second best swordsman: good, plays by the rules, the French

Ignorant antagonist: makes his own rules, like the Revolutionary Americans

As the experienced students marked up the quotation and reflected on it, they became aware that the best way to "discuss" it would be to explain the three character types and then relate them to some area they knew (here, the American Revolution). Those of us on the test development committee for a major nationwide test decided that we would even the field for the test takers and devise a precise directive that pointed out the most effective way to handle the question: "Write an essay that explains what Clemens means by his description of the 'best swordsman' and the 'ignorant antagonist.' Relate Clemens's concept to an area about which you are well informed." By giving these directions, we changed the examination from one testing students' experience with handling unclear essay questions to one testing their ability to write an essay handling complex concepts. The results still showed a great range of abilities, as the sample papers given in Chapter 4 demonstrate (beginning on p. 76), but the more precise question allowed the examination to elicit the information about the students that we really wanted.

Teachers helping students do their best on essay tests will use their knowledge about directives in two ways: to revise their own questions to make them more answerable, clearer, and more precise in their demands and to give students advice on and practice in responding to essay questions that are none of these and hence require that students construct a question before answering it.

It is often very difficult for teachers, who, as good test takers themselves, always understood the code terminology and readily constructed test questions to answer when necessary, to realize that many students simply do not understand what they are supposed to do in response to essay questions. The questions may seem obvious to initiates, but time spent in class on this issue will lead to much better essay test writing and greatly improved grades.

The Role of Memory

Most essay tests contain a hidden demand: to call material up from memory for the essay. Many students have a rich and full memory store, stocked with personal experiences, reading, history, arguments, and much more. Such students are never at a loss for a topic, though they often need help in organizing, focusing, and developing the material they have at the ready. Most essay questions simply assume that students have access to a rich store of material.

But many students do not have that access, nor do they have the background in remembered reading, intellectual conversation, and reflective introspection that the typical essay question draws on. This problem surfaces regularly in writing classes that focus on autobiography or other versions of personal experience, just as we see it in the uneven performance of students on personal-experience essay tests or those that draw on history that everyone supposedly knows. Because writing not only draws on but also increases memory, writing teachers ought to pay more attention to that relationship than other instructors do.

One strong argument for assigning personal-experience writing is that such writing enriches memory. As students learn to write about themselves, they gain new access to the materials of their own lives; it is common for an adult to comment, after writing a paper about a childhood experience, that only now does he or she really own the experience. In a similar way, the advocates of writing across the curriculum argue that the act of writing about anything gives ownership and immediacy to material that may have been distant and unrelated to the self. In short, we normally teach in our writing classes deep forms of understanding and learning, about the self and the subject. For many of our students, this use of writing to internalize and understand is novel and difficult; it also turns out to be profoundly instructive.

Essay testing is particularly frustrating for these students until they have learned how to call up from memory the events, details, and examples that are needed for most essay questions. Further, they will be expected to take an analytical and evaluative stance toward these memories, a stance that may seem unnatural to some who are not used to the academic culture. We ought to help such students understand and practice the kinds of memory exercises that most essay questions take for granted. One effective way to do this is through group discussion of responses to typical essay questions. Another way is to help students draw up lists of personal memories, historical references, and other matters likely to be of use on a particular test.

Let's use the Clemens question as an example. What historical events besides the American Revolution would illustrate (or argue against) the quotation? What personal experiences might the student be called on to use for the essay? (One student used a knowledge of chess to show that the quotation was dead wrong where skill alone mattered.)

WORKING WITHIN TIME CONSTRAINTS

The essential time problem with essay tests comes from the fact that most first-draft writing is usually faulty, disorganized, unclear, and unfocused. The secret to helping students do well on timed essay tests is to suggest ways, even under severe time limits, to hand in second or third drafts *without writing earlier drafts.* (The single greatest waste of time during an essay test comes from recopying drafts.) In other words, the good test taker will find a way to think through a first or discovery draft in scratch notes and then write a more finished draft in the time allowed. In addition, time must always be saved for rereading and editing during the last few minutes. Students should be encouraged to write on only one side of the page and write on every other line so that there will be plenty of room for neat revisions; they should also leave space at the start for a new opening to be written after the essay is finished.

This kind of time management ought not to be taken as only a test-taking skill. A pervasive problem with all kinds of writing is poor planning, which, for example, often leads to the late-night frenzy of writing still resorted to for too many term papers. Though different students will use different writing processes, a writing process that allows no time for revision usually produces weak work. As any writer with a deadline knows, planning is crucial for success. Most students will appreciate some help in planning for successful essay test writing, and experience with revision in the testing situation will carry over to more leisurely writing plans.

How long should an essay test take? Sometimes the institution establishes an exam schedule and the instructor must simply fit into the schedule. But often the teacher or test committee can design a time span that is appropriate for the purpose of the test. A test is, in one sense, a means of gathering information, and the time required for the test should depend on the complexity of the information being sought. Essay tests usually follow one of four patterns, which we will discuss in turn.

The Twenty-Minute Essay

Twenty-minute essay tests are designed to elicit two or three paragraphs that show mechanical competence and fluency. If the question is well constructed, it will allow students to begin writing almost immediately by drawing on personal experience or simple description and asking for a straightforward chronological structure. If the question is not clear, if it poses organizational problems, if it asks for much reflection, or if it makes other unreasonable demands for the time allowed, students will have to rewrite the question so that it can be answered in two or three paragraphs of hasty writing. Some students are very direct at doing this in their opening paragraphs: "I can't possibly write about the three most impressive teachers I have had, so let me tell you about my high school advanced placement teacher, who is the main reason I am now in college. . . ." It may seem risky to do this, but the people grading the test should recognize the good sense of accomplishing the possible, particularly if they are reading many essays that show the despair and confusion of attempting the impossible.

The Thirty-Minute Essay

In recent years, numbers of large-scale testing programs have begun to use the thirty-minute essay, often at the college graduation level; the best known are the California Basic Educational Skills Test (CBEST) for teacher candidates and the Medical College Admissions Test (MCAT). The time frame is administratively convenient, for two essays will fit neatly in one hour—the same reason essays of this length appear often on final examinations.

In contrast to the twenty-minute test, thirty minutes will allow for an organized and coherent essay of limited complexity. But successful students will need to manage their time with great care: five minutes or so for close reading of the question and brainstorming (on paper), another five minutes to arrange and focus the ideas (deciding on the one central idea the essay will demonstrate), fifteen minutes to write three or so focused paragraphs, and five minutes to edit and revise. Even with so little time, it is a good idea to write on every other line so that corrections and additions can be inserted neatly at the end of the time span.

The Forty-five-Minute Essay

Forty-five minutes remains the standard essay time span, and it allows for thoughtful, organized, and somewhat creative responses. The first ten minutes or so can be spent analyzing the question and outlining a response, almost half an hour can be spent writing, and time still remains for careful editing before the end of the test. Students should resist the impulse to recopy their drafts, which becomes more of a temptation as the time span increases; they should use all of the time allowed for organizing, writing, and editing. There is time to do extensive editing or even revision in the space between lines, on blank left-hand pages, and in the blank on the opening page. An opening paragraph that relates to the closing paragraph and points to the best ideas of the essay might, with luck, start the writing; more often, it should be written last.

Some instructors give their students a formula for writing the forty-five-minute essay, such as the "five-paragraph theme," a widely used strategy that can lead to limited success. This formula for writing essay tests requires that the student have three things to say about any topic, no more and no less; the first and last paragraphs list the three points, and the three middle paragraphs assert each idea and give a bit of evidence for each. The formula persists because it provides an easy, all-purpose organizational scheme; however forced or mechanical, it does help students who cannot come up with an organization that reflects what they have to say. Those who dislike the formula complain that it provides an organizational scheme as a substitute for having something to say and so discourages creative thinking. When students use the formula mechanically, they are likely to produce essays that stick out during essay readings like a mannequin on a cheerleading squad. Most students will have more or less than three things to say; some students will have nothing to say, and dividing nothing by five (paragraphs) still leaves nothing, despite the appearance of an essay. The strategy is particularly weak on development (it disallows more than one paragraph for each subtopic) and coherence (which it almost ignores), not to speak of its inappropriateness for some kinds of essay questions (such as comparison/contrast). But many instructors continue to teach it, on the grounds that some organizational scheme is preferable to none.

Instead of providing such formulas, teachers would be more helpful to students by offering them a range of organizational possibilities and idea-generating devices, recognizing that different students will learn and write in different ways. Some students will do best using formal outlines; others will be most productive using clustering (jotting down ideas any which way on the page and later organizing them with lines and circles); still others will profit from structured problem-solving mechanisms (heuristics). Some may even need to learn some stress-reducing techniques before they can begin to write well under time pressure.

The essays presented in Chapters 3 and 4 of this book were all written in forty-five minutes. Those at the top end of the scoring scale show how much can be said in this time span, if the time is well used.

One-, Two-, and Three-Hour Essays

As the time span increases, questions can become more complicated. A typical two-hour test, for example, may be an open-book question on essays read in advance, calling for detailed analysis of several of them, comparison and contrast, and connections to the student's experience. Curiously, writing quality does not seem to improve very much beyond that of the forty-five minute exam; the essays will simply be longer. Much of the additional time seems to be spent on worrying, rereading, and recopying of drafts.

Students taking long essay tests should spend the extra time thinking the question through and organizing their responses so that the draft they write will seem to be a second rather than first draft: It will be focused on a single controlling idea, organized around a sequence of connected assertions, and developed by use of examples and detail. In addition, students should save a substantial amount of time at the end for writing the first paragraph, revising the rest of the essay to develop and demonstrate the controlling idea, and editing it so that the essay they hand in is almost a third draft, despite the fact that it has been written and edited only once. The best preparation for such tests is extensive practice in organizing and revising complex papers.

ORGANIZING THE RESPONSE

Despite all the good advice about organizing writing on essay tests, very few students actually do it—so few, in fact, that it is worth trying to figure out why. I think that there are both theoretical and practical reasons for this resistance to a practice that would surely improve students' test writing and grades.

Some students have so little practice in reading and writing about ideas (as opposed to experiences) that a discussion of organization is premature. They need experience in reading and discussion to gain an understanding of ways to pursue ideas and arguments; they are likely to need help with invention and development strategies before there is much to organize. In spite of the fact that most students have plenty to say, some experience with exposition and argument, and a reasonable background of information to draw on, many have still not learned how to organize their writing.

Numbers of students have picked up a half-baked theory of writing, based on the muse theory of poetry: Either you will be inspired to write a terrific piece of first-draft writing, or you won't, and no amount of work will produce anything worth reading. In either case, there is no point in organizing or revising—in fact, such activities are an outrage to the muse, an attempt to impose reason on a mystical process.

Even without this dimly perceived romantic theory, most fluent college students see no point in organizing their work, for fluent first drafts (really discovery drafts) have often won them praise and high grades in the past. Too often, what has really mattered about writing has been correctness in mechanics and a certain amount of repetition of key ideas from the text or from lecture notes. When we speak of organizing thoughts and going through a series of drafts, we are changing the rules of a game that some students have learned to play successfully. "You can make me write," one student wrote on an essay test, "but you can't make me think!" We need to make clear that we are intentionally changing the rules. Avoiding thinking and revising may have been tolerated in the past, but writing and thinking now must go together; we must emphasize that organization and revision are an indispensable part of successful writing.

One good way to combat these destructive attitudes toward writing, I am convinced, is by way of assessment. Not until students have become able to distinguish good from weak responses will they realize that their work both needs improvement and can be improved with planning. They need to be exposed to scoring guides and other student papers, gradually internalizing critical standards that they can then begin to apply to their own work. And they need enough practice with revision to see that they are capable of recognizing their own best ideas, organizing them, providing evidence and connections for them, and rearranging them in improved order. In short, organization as a concept assumes that we are looking at writing as craftsmanship in critical thinking, not as inspiration or mechanics. Not until students have made that conceptual leap will advice on organization or practice in it have much effect.

Some teachers have found that regular practice in writing and writing assessment in class are the best means of helping students conceive of writing in this new way. If we value writing as a discovery process, which need not be organized or edited in preliminary form, we help students understand the difference between discovery drafts and finished drafts. A writing journal in which students both summarize and react to reading assignments, ungraded but collected and checked, is a powerful tool for reshaping attitudes about writing. Opening class with a "five-minute write," during which the pen must keep moving, can launch students directly into discussion. Such activities accustom students to writing as part of their regular thinking, talking, and reading activities and can help them understand the necessarily unshaped nature of draft writing. Materials such as journal entries and five-minute writes must be molded before they can become products submitted for grading. Peer grading and peer response sessions conducted in class when papers or drafts are due can open students' eyes to the possibilities of organized writing as critical thinking. Practice in writing timed tests and peer grading of those tests will reinforce the need for planning, organization, and revision.

The world seems filled with organizational schemes, and for a very good reason: People have a wide variety of ways of proceeding, depending to a great extent on their learning styles. Outlining works very well for those who proceed in a linear fashion, comfortable with categories and subcategories. But outlining feels like a straitjacket for other students, who need a more open and more holistic way of coming up with and arranging ideas.

We can help our students learn the most effective ways to organize their essays by giving them a series of options and by recognizing that our own way of organizing will not work for everyone. Besides outlining, we should be able to illustrate nonlinear procedures—clustering, cognitive mapping, listing of assertions, and other useful schemes for grouping and ordering ideas. Above all, we should demonstrate that only organization before writing will allow a student to write "second drafts" on essay tests, as there is never time to write two full drafts.

EDITING

It is important to distinguish editing from revising, a much more elaborate activity. During revision, we move paragraphs about, insert new pages, discard whole chunks of prose, reorganize, and come up with new ideas. Editing is a humble cousin of revision, though it may sometimes lead to revision. For example, work on sentence structure that is awry may reveal that the concept is poorly formed, and work on paragraph coherence may lead to revision of the paragraph, breaking it into two or more new ones. But in general, editing is the last phase of writing, a matter of tidying up the mechanics so that readers will not be distracted by errors or inconsistencies.

Not until we get to the forty-five-minute essay can we reasonably talk about revision; shorter essay tests simply do not allow time for that activity. (As mentioned earlier, this limitation of essay tests, which makes it difficult for writers to use an extended writing process to produce good drafts, has led to a recent emphasis on portfolio assessment; we return to this matter in Chapter 7.) So the final few minutes of every essay test should be spent on rereading and editing what has been written. Good writers will be able to do some revision, usually additions and deletions, as they edit, but most students should probably use this time for polishing and cleaning: inserting the occasional missing words typical of a hasty draft, correcting the inevitable spelling errors, replacing commas with semicolons where necessary, checking subject-verb agreement, and so on. No matter how much the grader of the essay tries to allow for hasty errors on exams, a cleaned-up paper will almost always receive a higher grade; some teachers find it extremely hard to respect the views of writers of error-filled prose, regardless of how intelligent the writing may be.

Some students want to bring dictionaries or thesauri to tests so that they can look up troublesome words. Though we must respect the impulse to use reference materials, they usually do more harm than good on timed essay tests.

The dictionary may help on spelling problems, but the time lost is usually not worth the improvement; in most cases, the presence of the dictionary suggests that the student should do editing while composing, instead of as a cleanup operation afterward, and the constant interruptions while writing destroy the essay. The thesaurus is even worse; it encourages the students to use longer and odder words rather than the clear ones they have in mind. There is so much to do during the usual timed essay test that reference books become distractions rather than supports. Some students feel so insecure without their references that it would be unsettling to forbid them, even on brief tests, but we might suggest that they are more helpful if left unopened during the limited time allowed for most essay tests. Not until we get into two-hour or longer tests will they be of much use.

During the past few years, the decreasing price and increasing power of laptop computers have made them more available for students taking essay tests. These portable machines will surely become more and more common as time goes on. Students with various disabilities are now using them to great purpose. Perhaps as they become more common, with their increasingly sophisticated word processing capabilities (including dictionaries, thesauri, spelling checkers, and grammar checkers), efficient editing will become such a routine part of essay test writing that it will no longer affect grading. Then we will be able to focus, as we should, on what the student has to say and how it is organized, developed, and expressed.

Computers have the potential for changing writing assessment in many additional ways. Like the typewriter, whose advocates predicted conceptual revolutions from writing by machine, the computer does ask writers to compose in a different way than the pen does; every experienced writer knows that word processing aids revision and increases production. Nonetheless, I am a bit skeptical that the newer machine will in fact alter student essay test writing substantially. But unlike the typewriter, computers can also alter the way we read and respond to writing when we are not under time pressure. Some writing classes in well-equipped schools are using bulletin boards and E-mail systems as part of the writing process, with provisions for constant and wide-ranging responses from readers, and more and more writing classes are now being taught in computer labs.

It is possible that new assessment devices will emerge from such practices; it is even possible that computer writing may lead to some kind of computer scoring. I have not seen much evidence yet for the usefulness of these innovations for assessment, though they do have their enthusiastic supporters. In fact, some contrary evidence is starting to accumulate that the computer spell checkers and style checkers actually decrease the overall quality of student impromptu writing, for they direct attention away from the flow of ideas to word-level concerns. The clarity of the papers when printed is sometimes misleading and students may mistakenly take pride in a neat-looking product when proof of a well-developed writing process is what is sought.

Essay test scores ought to reflect how well students think and how well they can put this thinking into organized prose. Instructors complain about tests and resent that their good students may sometimes test poorly. But with essay tests, instructors can make direct connections between the writing instruction and assignments that they give their students and the tests that these students normally take outside of the writing class. Most students will be writing essay tests, and much is at stake in their performances on such tests. For this reason, writing courses ought to help students learn how to do well on essay tests.

CHAPTER 3

PLACEMENT OR DIAGNOSTIC ESSAY TESTS BASED ON PERSONAL EXPERIENCE

───────────────⟨⟩───────────────

IS PLACEMENT A GOOD IDEA?

The first English placement test for entering college students was given at Harvard University in 1874. The test seems to have had two major functions: to blame the schools for failing to prepare students adequately for the most selective of universities and to maintain the class structure at Harvard by humiliating students who did not show upper-class linguistic manners. The test also played a role in shifting the teaching of writing from the university faculty, which had traditionally spent much of their time working with student writing, to a temporary (and less well paid) teaching staff. The test sent an important message that writing was now to be considered preparation for college work, not a substantial part of college work. The faculty at the time, of course, did not see the test that way at all; they felt it was a crucial means of maintaining standards and of helping students succeed.

These contrasting views are evident today in the continuing controversy over student placement. Some faculty and administrators regard placement testing as indefensible negative labeling that segregates some students from

45

regular college work, while others consider placement as the most effective way to keep standards high in the freshman English course and to help students gain the skills they need if they are to make it through the first year. Some institutions go through regular cycles of introducing and then abandoning placement as one or the other view predominates. American higher education as a whole has gone through such a cycle in the past generation, with many colleges abandoning placement testing (along with part or all of freshman English) in the 1960s, reestablishing the programs during the 1970s, and now in the 1990s again contemplating the abolition of placement.

Each college and university should consider the question of placement in light of its own student body and its own writing curriculum. Placement makes sense if two conditions are present: a significant number of students who are failing—or are likely to fail—the freshman course because their entering-level skills are inadequate and a remedial or developmental program with sufficient funding and staff to help those students succeed. On the one hand, evidence shows that when those two conditions prevail, as they do in many public institutions, placement testing and support programs will in fact dramatically increase the number of poorly prepared students who succeed in college. It is also clear that when very weak students are present in the freshman English class, they demand a disproportionate amount of teacher time and lower the overall expectations of the course. On the other hand, there is surely a price to be paid, in the low morale of students—not to speak of teachers—assigned to such programs as a result of failing the test and being labeled "boneheads." When relatively few such students are present, placement may not be worth the price; with all students in freshman English, teachers using diagnostic testing can identify those needing special help, which may be provided by a writing lab or tutorial center. Further, all too many developmental courses are poorly funded, out of date, and inadequately staffed; the second-rate treatment of developmental teachers and students sometimes adds insult rather than support to the students most in need.

Nonetheless, a substantial majority of American colleges and universities undertake placement testing, expecting that it will enhance the quality of the freshman course and help low-scoring students succeed over time. Because instructional time is very expensive, any test that places students in the right course on the first day of classes turns out to be highly cost-effective for the university. When done properly, placement testing wins the assent of most students, for this form of institutional caring places them where they can learn the most and be successful. This chapter and the next will assume that your institution has reviewed the issue, that it has decided to institute a placement test, and that it has established (as it then must) a program specifically designed to help students who are designated by the test as needing additional instructional support.

CRITERIA FOR A PLACEMENT OR DIAGNOSTIC TEST

When you serve on a committee responsible for a placement test, you want to know if each student has the skills to profit from the course subject to placement, usually required freshman English. Because every college is somewhat different from every other, you need to create a list of skills appropriate for your own situation. A highly selective school, for example, might ask entering first-year students for considerable background in reading, control over sentence and paragraph structure, an extensive vocabulary, and a developed writing process. Such a background allows the freshman course to ask for complicated reading assignments, consideration of a variety of ways to demonstrate (rather than merely to assert) ideas, and individualized research projects. An open-admission community college, by contrast, must plan for a different kind of background. In this situation, you may want to see if students are familiar with the differences between oral and written dialects, have become accustomed to meeting assigned topics, have enough self-confidence to write with their own voice, and have sentence sense.

In American higher education, there is no consistent definition of remedial or developmental English; every institution must define for itself what readiness for freshman English in fact means. In every placement decision you will want to be alert for those whose writing abilities have been cramped by overattention to correctness in early stages of the writing process or who feel that writing is only a patterned game of filling in the blanks (as in a multiple-choice test or the five-paragraph theme) or whose skill at composition is partly obscured by inappropriate use of the spoken dialect in school writing. Some students may require special tutorial assistance or even a prior course (if available), and the sooner you find out these limitations, the better. The basic question you are asking is "Is each student sufficiently ready for what the first-year course will be teaching that success is both possible and probable?"

One institutional decision becomes critical if a placement test is to be effective: Teachers of freshman English must agree with some specificity on the goals for the course and on what they can reasonably expect of entering students. If every instructor has an independent curriculum and individual goals—as is sometimes the case—placement testing makes no sense because it is impossible to devise criteria. But the goals of the freshman writing course should be determined by the institution, and standards should be reasonably consistent from section to section. For these reasons, some institutions will use the introduction of a placement test as one generally effective means of initiating a conversation on the purposes of the freshman writing course.

Essay test scoring for placement purposes usually requires a holistic reading that ranks students from high to low score so that those at the low end of the scale can be placed in a remedial or developmental course. Scoring for diagnostic testing might also take place with a focused holistic or primary-trait essay reading, or it may simply be done by the teacher of the class, depending on the use to which the scoring will be put. For example, if the assessment will determine which students receive tutorial or writing lab assistance, a reliable test score from an essay reading will be most appropriate; it is an institutional judgment. But if the results will be used to guide special writing assignments and conferences with the teacher, a teacher's grade is most appropriate. (More details on essay test scoring will be given later in this chapter.)

If you are teaching a developmental or remedial writing course, you have a special problem: Developmental students are accustomed to thinking of themselves as inept in English classes or even stupid. They expect the diagnostic test to prove that they don't know grammar (and never will), and they envision the course as a discouraging grind. Perhaps you do, too. The placement test and the course share this problem: They must both focus on writing as well as thinking and on ways to improve writing and thinking. If either the test or the course becomes a mechanical exercise, the attempt to use placement to help students succeed will be doomed.

A diagnostic essay test may not lead to placement of students, though it sometimes does, but is usually intended to elicit information about the students' abilities and needs so that the work in class can be specifically designed for individual students and, under the best circumstances, will help them succeed.

DESIGNING OR SELECTING A PLACEMENT OR DIAGNOSTIC TEST

Many colleges are accustomed to using a multiple-choice editing test as a diagnostic or placement test for the writing course. Commercial testing firms assiduously promote such tests as a low-cost and efficient placement device. But every teacher and administrator should be aware of the limitations of multiple-choice tests of editing skills. Although the editing tests do correlate to some degree with real writing for white, middle-class speakers of Standard English (see Edward M. White, *Teaching and Assessing Writing,* 2nd. ed. San Francisco: Jossey-Bass, 1994. 171–96), the correlations are much weaker for students who come from other racial and social categories or who speak other varieties of English. And now that most composition courses teach a writing process that puts editing at the end of a string of activities, the skills tested are typically taught at the end; most courses now begin with a writing assignment rather than editing. Further, a placement or diagnostic test conveys a message about the substance of college composition. If the test measures only editing skills, using a multiple-choice format, the message sent to high schools is that college writing requires students to learn to choose (or to guess) a single right answer among a series of wrong ones. However, if the test asks students to write, it tells the schools to prepare their students to generate ideas, read critically, and plan thoughtfully. Most colleges prefer the second message.

A diagnostic writing assignment based on personal experience, such as the two given in this chapter, has several other benefits. Because it asks students to draw from and reflect on their personal experience, every student should have plenty to write about and should be interested in the topic. Even very weak writers can accomplish some description, and very good writers will have a chance to manage tone and point of view for subtle effects. This kind of personal-experience topic is also good preparation for expository writing because the use of concrete detail as evidence for what the writer has to say reinforces the need to demonstrate ideas. In addition, you can see if the student is accustomed to understanding and fulfilling writing goals and if the student has a writing process that he or she can describe. (The essay test offers a starting point for entries into students' writing logs.) Editing problems are sure to appear, if you want to begin attending to them right away. But as we will demonstrate in our discussion of the unsuccessful paper, the editing problems are part of an entire process that requires attention.

If you prefer to use a more expository and text-based assignment for the placement or diagnostic essay, several options appear in Chapter 4.

ESSAY TEST 1: PERSONAL-EXPERIENCE ASSIGNMENT 1

Describe a person you knew well when you were a child. Your object is to use enough detail that your readers can picture the person clearly from the child's perspective and at the same time understand from the tone of your description and from the particular details you choose how you felt about the person you describe.

If you are using this assignment as a test, you will, of course, print it for all students taking the test. Many teachers will be more casual about their assignments in class, but it is generally good practice, and most efficient, to duplicate and distribute all class assignments. Many students will not take notes if you merely tell them what you are expecting, and they will take your assignments more seriously if you provide them with a hard copy. If you assign the paper to be written at home, you should also spend a considerable amount of time discussing the assignment with students and reminding them to take notes on the sheet you have distributed so that the information they need will be at hand when they start writing.

Your discussion of the assignment should focus on the key words, as we noted in Chapter 2. *Describe* suggests concrete detail, for example; you may want to help students see the difference between vague and telling detail: "Her crooked smile never left her lips" is much more effective than "she was a friendly person." Some students will ask how old the child in the assignment is expected to be. You might reply that any age will do, as long as there is some distance from the present; the student will need to choose a specific age, stick with it, and be sure to give the reader sufficient clues. You should also point out that you do not want the child's language, merely the child's perspective. And the challenge of the assignment should be stressed: Can you let us know just how you felt only by description, without telling us directly? Depending on your class, you might want to let that instruction stand as a kind of game, or you may want to press further into the concept of *tone*.

Tone has to do with the relation of writer to reader and of writer to topic (sometimes also called mood). The concept is not complicated; it insists that all writing is an act of communication and hence involves some kind of relationship. Your students know about tone in conversation. They might describe their friends as "husky" or "chunky," whereas people they don't like are "fat." They may have studied something called "connotation" and "denotation" in school. But the tone of writing is set in many ways besides the use of metaphors and connotations: Such matters as abrupt or leisurely sentences, direct or indirect quotation, and even punctuation help determine the relationship of writer to reader. The issue here is that students select actively (rather than passively) the right words and sentences, with the right tones, to express the relationship they have in mind in the assignment.

If you use this first essay as a timed diagnostic test, you will probably not be able to have the prewriting discussion described here before the test; you will be testing to see if the students can go about these procedures on their own. But you may want to give the students an opportunity to revise their work after you return it to them, scored, as a springboard for instruction in such matters as tone or revision. I suggest that you duplicate and distribute the scoring guide and the sample papers illustrating it on the next pages in this chapter, if you use them to guide your scoring; they will help demonstrate differences in quality, illustrate the clarity and fairness of the grading, and reinforce the need and possibilities for revision. The discussion can then be particularly rich and fruitful.

Though you may not wish to grade the essay for class purposes, sometimes it is necessary to do so for other reasons; you may be using the results for placement or be giving a pretest/posttest to your students to evaluate how much they learn by the end of the term. That is, you may want to give the essay test again at the end of the term to see if students have learned how to write this kind of assignment more effectively. If so, you will need to compare student scores. If you are giving the diagnostic essay to a large group (the entire entering first-year class, for instance), you will want to conduct a holistic scoring session to obtain the most reliable test scores for rankings. The sample scoring guide for this question that follows can be used by a group of instructors, or even students, as well as by the individual instructor; it is based on the kind of scoring that many large-scale testing programs use.

The holistic scoring guide is based on several principles. At its core, it assumes that writing is best judged as a whole rather than as a series of discrete skills. We need to teach separate skills, of course, and to notice which aspects of writing a particular class may need to focus on. But for scoring purposes, holistic theory says that the whole is greater than the sum of its parts and that readers respond to overall quality.

You will also notice that this scoring guide, and those that follow, use numbers rather than the conventional letter grading scale. Two principles lie behind the use of numbers for grading: Such a system leads to more consistent scoring in large groups (where different faculty bring wholly different concepts about the meaning of, say, an "A" grade); students will also respond less emotionally to numbers than to letters, which for many have come to reflect their worth as students (or even as people) rather than the quality of a writing draft. Each of the scoring guides in this book is based on a 6-point scale, with 6 as the highest score. This scale has been found to be useful both for large-scale scoring and for classroom instruction. The scoring guides in this chapter and the next do vary according to the writing assignment, and you (or your department, as a group) should not hesitate to change them if they do not seem to fit your students. Scoring guides must be appropriate to both the assignment and the students. However, if you are attempting to measure the difference between a pretest and a posttest, be sure to use the same scoring guide for both tests.

Holistic Scoring Guide

Students should be rewarded for what they do well in response to the question. In timed first-draft writing, every writer will make a few errors. *Patterns* of errors, such as repeated failures to predicate sentences or to relate ideas, will usually indicate a lower-half essay (scored 3, 2, or 1), but occasional errors are likely to appear in even the best writing. Evaluate the essay as a whole, without giving undue weight to any single aspect.

Here the student is asked to *describe* a particular person, using detail, so that a reader can understand the nature of the relationship. Essays that do not select a particular person or that are so general in their descriptions that we must guess at the relationship should be scored in the lower half, as they fail to understand and respond to the question.

6. A **superior** response will not only define and describe the person in detail but also provide vivid and particular descriptions arranged for a clear purpose. It will have a personal voice and use words with attention to their tone as well as their meaning; it will have a discernible organization and be focused.

5. The **strong** response will be less vivid, detailed, and focused than the superior one and may explain the relationship as well as show it. But the writing will accomplish the task strongly; the paper will use words with care and be orderly.

4. The **competent** response will accomplish the task in a minimal way: The descriptions will be clear enough to convey a relationship, but not in a particularly distinct way; the writing is likely to be marked by minor but frequent errors.

3. The **weak** response does not accomplish the task, for a variety of reasons: It tells about, rather than describes, a person; it features minimal or muddled detail; it loses track of its purpose; it shows patterns of error.

2. The **inadequate** response is likely to show patterns of serious error, to misunderstand or confuse the question, to use superficial and stereotyped language, to include oral structures with the written language, or otherwise demonstrate serious problems.

1. The **incompetent** response conveys ineptness at handling the assignment: It reflects failed attempts to begin the task, inability to produce the written dialect, unwillingness to undertake the writing assignment, and the like.

If you were to use this scoring guide for the sample essays that follow, you would have to adapt it somewhat for your particular situation. The scores should represent reasonable levels of accomplishment for your particular school, and those levels of accomplishment should reflect the kind of writing your students normally produce. Successful essays will probably fit into the 6–5 range; marginal essays, in the 4–3 range; and unsuccessful essays, the 2–1 range. You should have enough representative papers at hand to allow you to make decisions about the scoring scale and about the applicability of the various levels for the sample essays before you begin grading.

Sample Student Essays

Score of 6

A Fourth-Grade Memory

Looking back, practically the first thing I think of when I remember her is her behind. It was a ponderous specimen

to the fourth grader that I was; always an impossible
obstacle thrust out into the aisles of our desks as she leaned
on her elbows, absorbed in the smudgy penciled work of one of
her students. I would stand contemplating it, wrapping one
white knee-socked leg around the other, waiting. It was not
that she intimidated me—she that sat in the dirt of our
playground as if she were one of us—I could have made my need
to pass known, but where, where to poke or tap her? Her
shoulders were bowed over the desk, her face beaming not two
inches away from her pupil's.

Her face was an entirely different matter. The
precision of her nose brought to mind the image of a pert
little bird, a sparrow perhaps. Her eyes were a crisp blue,
literally framed by scholarly brown glasses. Her hair might
have reminded a student or two of the pictures of the thatched
roofs in Norway that she enthusiastically waved at us during
geography hour. (She once confided to me that she looked in
the mirror but once a day, exclaiming, ''God, you're
gorgeous!'' and then abandoned vanities for the rest of the
day.)

Despite her decrepitude—she must have been over forty
years old—she was a real Bohemian, complete with bean bag
chairs and tie-dyed blouse. She had a deep affection for my
father. She was widowed or divorced, I suppose, with three
teen-aged children, and when she asked me how my father was
and told me that he had the most beautiful, happy eyes, I
wanted to hug her and let her move into my room with me. She
must have been very lonely.

She was generally a soft-spoken person, but was capable

of an awesome bellow that would stop any taunting boy in his cruel tracks. How often I wanted to bury my head in her polyester lap, my friend, my protector, but she was my teacher. I respected her not only wholly, but voluntarily.

Score of 5

Someone

He was someone who sat at our dinner table and told us to ''shut-up'' so he could listen to the news; he told us to eat our vegetables or we would get no dessert. He was someone who caused me to cry and leave the table if I spilled some milk because I so wanted to please him. He was someone I said goodbye to at night when he went off to work. He was someone who got us up in the morning and told us to get ready for school and ''Be sure to make your beds,'' he always said. I remember him helping me do my math problems, and how I would get upset when he would yell at me because I could not understand. He was always telling me to straighten my room, hang the clothes, do the dishes, and help your mom with dinner.

He was someone whom my mom would ask to take us somewhere on Sunday. He was always telling us kids to be quiet and not to fight while he was driving. He once stopped at a wreck and showed us what might happen if we did not behave while he was driving. He was someone who broke my arm by shaking me and swinging me on the ground when my younger sister and I were fighting. He was someone who gave us an allowance so we could go to the show on Saturday.

He was someone who worked hard for our food and clothes, and who on Sundays at my mom's request took us somewhere.

I am still trying to please my father and wishing he were different than he is. He is someone whom I respect for his hard work, but I wish he would please me more with himself. Today my father and I talk of troubles in the world, but never of any personal troubles or concerns. He is still the someone who tells us, "Be quiet!" at the dinner table whenever we are home to eat. He is still the someone who furnishes us with food and a place to sleep; but now he never offers us a dime unless we ask. He no longer takes us somewhere on Sundays because our family cannot get along.

My father will always be someone whom I respect, but he will never be the dad I have always admired and wished was my own.

Score of 4 or 3

Gramps

Gramps, we called him. My mother's father was very old, but always enjoyed seeing us kids when we came for summer visits. He lived alone in a small town in Ohio, I don't remember the name, in a small house with a garden out back.

Gramps loved to work in the garden and he always had things for us to do. How he kept his pipe going all day long while weeding I'll never know. Once he showed us how the irragation worked and I helped him cut and put in a new line. He never seemed to lose patience, though I'm sure I was not much help.

He always had a housekeeper, though I don't remember
much about them. Somehow, food appeared at mealtime and the
house was clean. When we were there Gramps spent all his time
with us, though we were always helping him do his chores. The
special time of the day was walking downtown to get an ice
cream cone on hot afternoons. At night he liked to read
stories to us from an old dusty book.

Gramps died a few years ago, I really did not pay much
attention at the time, I was busy with school and sports. But
now as I write this I realize that I miss him for lots of
reasons and wish I had appreciated him more.

Score of 2

Desert Home

As a child, my parents moved from Texas to California in
search for a better paying job. My parents had no idea of
living in the desert would be like, yet my father had high
hopes because among his friends he heard that California was
the place to live, and jobs were more available. As time went
by, my parents soon learned that the lower desert in Southern
California was a rough rugget, bold place to live. The dry
climate was very hot in the summer and very cold in winter.
The large stretches of land made the desert spacious. So
roomy that people felt lonely when left alone unvisited by
civilization.

As a rule everyone knew and respected owning a car or
truck in the desert. It was a major prority or else suffer the
consequences of being stranded out without transportation

which made life even more miserable. On paid days, once a
month, the whole community rised from the dead in an up roar
of happiness. Everyone knew their destination. Some headed
towards Needles, other to 29 palms, Barstow, and San
Bernardino. Leaving the desert for awhile, and coming in
contact with civilization again meant alot for the 15
families that worked for Santa Fe Railroad Company.

Our small community was called Cadiz, California. It
had a post office a train station, a small market called
Champlus, a tailer park, and eight cabins for visitors
stopping off from highway 66, a gasoline station, and a
restaurant that was a couple miles away. You see! route 66 was
the main road to civilization.

Discussion of the Essays

I suggest that you begin responding to the assignment by asking your students
to consider the importance of understanding what a writing assignment calls
for. Students need to see that the central concern of this particular topic is the
use of detail to meet the goals of the assignment. Many students write inadequate
essays because they do not pay enough attention to the job at hand. The first
successful response does depart from the descriptive goal of the assignment to
discuss the relationship in its last sentence, as does the second one. But the
second essay uses powerful detail to convey the distant and disappointingly
harsh relationship between the writer and the father, brilliantly conveyed by
the "Someone" of the title. The first essay, by a more talented writer, handles
the assignment with great sophistication, managing language and point of view
with skill. The writer of the 4/3 response understands that detail is necessary
but gives the detail in a scattered way, not focusing on any particular aspect
of the relationship.

The writer of the 2 essay loses track of both the topic and the goal of the
assignment. This student has some feel for the language of description but is
not accustomed to the school dialect; at numerous places, the writer uses a
rough approximation of oral dialect (*rugget, paid days, couple miles*), and the

student is unlikely to know how to revise or edit. What can you do to help this student without overwhelming her with everything that is wrong with the paper?

The writer of this essay needs to see that she did not meet the goal of the assignment in that she describes a town rather than a person. She must also be told that she will have to develop a writing process that will allow for revision and editing to bring her initial ideas into the school dialect. The writing indicates a paucity of experience with writing assignments, experience that assessment will help her gain and that she must have if she is to succeed.

What resources are available at your institution to help such a student? Is there a remedial program that will help her learn what she needs to know? Can she be assigned a tutor in the learning center? regular conferences with you? a peer tutor from the class itself? Your objective as a teacher is to read this student's errors as an indication of ways to provide help, rather than merely as an indication of failure.

You will, of course, want to use this essay assignment in various ways in addition to its placement or diagnostic function. Students should begin their writing logs by describing how they went about producing the paper; if you ask them to revise the essay (always a good idea), a description of the process of revision should also go into the log. Depending on your class and your institution, you may want to deal with organization of the paragraph and the essay as a whole, with sentence structure, or with other issues that have emerged. And you will want to distinguish this kind of assignment from more analytical and expository essays to follow.

ESSAY TEST 2: PERSONAL-EXPERIENCE ASSIGNMENT 2

Many observers of our society claim that modern people, immersed in materialism, are "owned by their objects." Yet many of us have objects that we treasure not just for their material value but for a variety of other reasons. Describe one object that is important to you. Explain what values it represents, and comment on those values.

This topic is parallel to the first diagnostic essay in its demands. It requires detailed description, draws on the writer's experience for subject material, and moves beyond mere description into levels of abstraction. The difference between the two topics, however, may be significant for some students. Many students find it easier to describe objects than people, and such students will perform more successfully on this topic. Similarly, because a discussion of values is a more straightforward activity than management of tone, this topic will be easier for students without much control of verbal nuance. Nonetheless, the challenge of recalling human relationships may stimulate certain introspective students to write more effectively on the first assignment, despite the fact that it is in one sense more difficult. And some students may write badly on the second assignment because they may be unable to discuss values without resorting to simple sentimentalism or stock phrases.

This topic is built on the usual test demand for a well-stocked and accessible bank of memories. Even more than most, it calls for students to come up with a suitable memory, decked out with detail, before they can begin to compose. The student who came up with the music box as object (the 6 paper that follows) clearly had an advantage over the student whose memory could supply only the clichéd teddy bear. Every essay question contains this kind of hidden demand for memory and for retrieval of the right kind of memory for the writer's use. Nearly all questions, even text-based ones, will ask for details, support, or examples as part of the response.

If you choose to discuss this topic with your students before they write, you will probably want to spend time considering the most appropriate objects they might choose. Most students, particularly in a test situation, just plunge in, writing about the first thing that comes to mind. More skillful students, however, will pause before beginning to write, choosing from a range of possibilities.

It is also effective to assign the topic as a diagnostic test without prior discussion and then to discuss these matters with the students after you return their first attempts, as they begin their revisions. Here is a scoring guide to use (or adapt) for this assignment.

Holistic Scoring Guide

As with the first assignment, students should be rewarded for what they do well in response to the question. Here they are asked to *describe* an object important to them. They are further asked to *explain* what values it represents and to comment on those values. Note that the question does not ask for unusual objects. But it does require the choice of a specific object, not generalized abstractions such as life or God, and it asks for some descriptive detail as well as a more abstract discussion of values.

6. A **superior** response will not just name an object but will also describe it in some detail, and the essay will not just identify the values represented but will explain and comment on them, their nature, and their source. A superior essay will be literate and orderly, despite the occasional minor error.

5. The **strong** response will both describe a particular object and explain the values it represents, but without the unusual richness and development of the 6 essay.

4. The **competent** response will select and describe an object, though less fully than the 5 essay; it will adequately consider the issue of values. Minor mechanical or grammatical errors may be noticeable but do not seriously distract the reader.

3. The **weak** response may adequately handle both parts of the assignment but will contain too many mechanical or grammatical errors to be considered competent. It may be mechanically competent but fail to accomplish the task, for example, by dealing with only one part of the two-part question, ignoring the representativeness of specific objects, or treating the subject in superficial, immature, or stereotyped fashion.

2. The **inadequate** response is likely to show patterns of serious error, to misunderstand or confuse the question, to use superficial and stereotyped language, to show consistent oral interference with the written language, or otherwise demonstrate serious problems.

1. The **incompetent** response conveys ineptness at handling the assignment: It will reflect failed attempts to begin the task, inability to produce the written dialect, unwillingness to undertake the writing assignment, and the like.

Sample Student Essays

Score of 6

The Music Box

We have in our living room a music box, which for three generations has given pleasure to the eyes and ears of my family. It stands about a foot high and measures about two feet in length and width. Except for a spray of flowers carved on its face, the outside is unadorned. Inside, pasted to the

lid, is a turn-of-the-century lithograph of a pair of plump
cherubs. There is a set of tin records, perforated here and
there, that goes with the music box. It is run by winding it
up and releasing the spring. Its tunes are dated; ''My Gal Is
A High-Born Lady'' and ''I Guess I'll Telegraph My Baby''
haven't been among the top ten for quite a while, but this
does nothing to lessen the enjoyment they give.

My grandfather was the first to own the music box. He
traded a horse for it and presented the music box to my
grandmother as a gift. They had been married for only six
months. At first it was a very big deal. A music box in a
Nebraskan farming town can cause quite a commotion, but as
time went by and the popularity of ''victrolas'' grew, the
music box passed into oblivion.

Ignored and dusty was the way my father discovered it in
the cellar. He cleaned it up and got it running and showed it
off patronizingly to his friends as a relic from his parent's
youth. It was played at parties as a novelty, but again it lost
out against the incoming rage: the radio. So back into the
cellar went the music box to await rediscovery one more time.

This time it was my sister and I who resurrected it. We
hauled it out into the light, dusted off its rosewood sides
and listened to the songs first heard what seemed to us to be
eons ago.

My grandparents grew old, and being practical people,
decided to divide their possessions with their children
before their death to avoid a tragic scramble afterwards. To

my father went the music box, and he carefully brought it to our home and revived it one more time.

Now, despite its years, it keeps on playing its old familiar songs. I love the old music box. It can never be associated with a price tag. My grandfather acquired it with an honest trade and it has been handed down through the years. The music box symbolizes my grandfather's love for my grandmother, my father's years at home, my sister and I exploring in the dark cellar and countless fine memories. I love it for its beauty, the rich, soft red of the rosewood, the way it gleams in the sun. I love the whirr of the motor and vigorously cranking the handle. I love the corny song titles and running my fingers over the rough surface of the records. And although its value is largely sentimental, its worth stems from the fact that it has survived many years with grace and beauty; something very few *people* can claim.

Score of 5

My House

As I look back on my life, the object that I place the most value on is the house that I grew up in. For sixteen years I walked through its doors and lived in its rooms. That house became a part of me.

Now, almost nineteen years old, it stands in a middle-class suburb of Los Angeles. The surrounding streets are lined with well-kept homes and neatly trimmed yards.

Children that I don't know play baseball on the avenue

and cars that I don't recognize fill the driveways. My dear
house is in an alien world both to me and to it.

My family took pride in that home. We bought it new, put
in all the landscaping, and made it a beautiful place to live.
In all the years we lived there, I never once took its
loveliness for granted. I would sit and look at it and know
what a wonderful home we had.

That long avenue was my world. Little playmates moved in
and out of the other houses, but I was the stable one. I
didn't believe we would ever leave our home.

That building saw my first step, heard my first word,
and watched me fall off of my first bicycle. It stood by when
I was sick and was there for all the happy moments too. It
became more like a person, part of the family.

Leaving it all alone for new people to run about in was
next to impossible. Is it as lonely as I am?

Our new house is bigger and more modern than that one
was. Still, this makes no difference. It will never be home.

Score of 4

Objects I Value

At this point in life, I don't have many objects which I
value a great deal. The few things I do value have a
sentimental value rather than a monetary value.

The first objects I value are trophies I won diving.
They have a very deep sentimental value to me because it was
my reward for the hours and years I practiced, working for a
goal. When I look at my trophies on the shelf I think of all

the joys I felt at winning and also the heart break of losing. I think of the self-control and self-discipline I gained at going to practice each day while my friends were at the beach. This, right now, is very important to me. These trophies have no real monetary value or sentimental value to anyone but me because only I earned these trophies and only I cherish them.

Another object which I value is a ring I recieved from my grandmother. This ring is also a sentimental object to me. I recieved it after she passed away and so it is my rememberance of her. This ring also has monetary value. It is a gold ring with a small diamond in it. Others would value it because of it's worth but my family and I are the only ones who value it for a sentimental reason.

My next valuable object is my wallet. My value on my wallet is very sentimental. In it, it contains all my pictures of friends and experiences which I have gone through. If someone stole my wallet or I lost it, I would rather lose my money than some of the pictures inside. Maybe this is because I am not overflowing with money at the moment but right now my pictures come over my money.

My last valuable is a watch I received at Christmas from my boyfriend. This is very important to me because it is from him. I have had watches before from my parents and they really didn't have very much sentimental value to them. But my watch contains many memories and I would really be upset if I misplaced it. Just like the ring, it is valuable to others because of the cost but to me it is the person who it signifies.

These are my most valuable objects and it isn't because
of the amount of money they're worth but instead for the
sentimental value of them. I don't really own anything
excessively expensive so I really don't value many things for
their value in money.

Score of 3

Bear—Bear

Blue body with a white tummy and round black eyes, soon
to be loved. This poor little teddy bear went through so much
just for me.

When I came home after my birth, I had 3 sisters and a
strange new friend waiting for me. My sister Jamie had a teddy
bear placed in my crib. They tell me I actually giggled when I
first saw *my* teddy bear.

Well days went on and after countless washings, due to
being thrown-up on or thrown into the toilet, my little teddy
bear had seen his last day with those round black eyes. Yes,
my little teddy bear needed some new eyes and blue buttons, so
Jamie did a repair job, with some grown-up help. Now it seemed
perfect. After all, blue eyes match a blue body!

Jamie decided, one day, that she would teach me how to
say Teddy Bear. It was a noble effort on her part even though
all I could repeat was *Bear*! The Teddy bear still didn't have
a name.

The next day when I was in the living room, I realized
that my teddy bear wasn't around. With the terrifying thought

that he might be gone, my tiny voice piped up with; ''Bear—Bear, Bear—Bear!''

There was no mistaking what I wanted. Now that he had a name, Bear—Bear would never be more than a helping hand away.

I never really pondered on why I kept Bear—Bear all these years. It's simple——I love him and I'll keep him many more years I imagine. Bear—Bear will always mean love, security, and friendship. Perhaps that's why I choose my friends carefully and value their love so greatly. My friends have been wonderfully good to me (and vise—versa) since the very first time my giggle said ''Hi, let's be friends!''

Score of 2

Cars

Heat, exhaust, fumes, burning rubber and smoke are all caused by a remarkable invention that has spured our society into being one of the most materialistic in this modern age. Our society today depends on the car for transportation. We overlook the bad side of this invention for all the wonderful things the car has done for us.

No longer are people confined to one small region for their entire lives. Trips to the coast or to a distant city for a day are not unheard of now. It has actually broadened our horizons for we can meet new people, go new places. People we haven't seen in along time are in easy reach.

Working days are shortened with the use of the car. Instead of walking many miles to work, it provides fast and easy transportation on highways.

Status is related to owning a car. Some people seem to feel that the bigger a car is, the better it is. Socio-economic status is based on the number of high value materialistic things we own. Having four or five cars in a family tends to raise a family's status.

Cars come in all shapes and sizes. Big or small we can find one that fits the needs of everybody. Compact, economy and luxary cars are priced to fit people with even low income budgets as well as high.

There is a limit that people using cars must draw. Excessive use of a car can damage our enviornment. Taking a car into high mountain area can damage or even ruin flora and fauna. Pollution from cars cannot be stopped unless all cars are banned.

With all the good and bad sides to cars, which way can we turn? Cars can be used for destructive purposes as well as useful, meaningful reasons.

Score of 1

My Values

I am going to write on some object which are pretty important to me. The first would be my religion because I think I should put my faith in something other than ''man,'' and worldly goods. I also believe that I as a person have that right to look forward to something bigger and better in life, I can live life better day by day. This is important because I'm a person who doesn't like to have things cramed down my throat then expected to digest it easily. I feel I have the right to choose who and what I believe in, without someone handing me 2 alternatives to chose from. I want to choose freely on my own will and judgment. I feel that I am old enough to choose and have ''free choice.'' Another object or value which is important to me is my ''Freedom.'' I like to do what I like, go where I want, see what I want, to a point where I do not interfer with another persons ''Freedoms.'' My whole life is based on what I can do for me and other people. Without this freedom I could not serve to the best of my ability my fellow man. I couldn't put forth 100% because I would be restricted to do only certain things. Therefore, without my religion and freedom to do what I want I should have never have been born and with out these two basics of life I do not see how any man can live. So I have told you two of my basic values, again they are ''Freedom to choose my own religion'' and basic Freedom to live an everyday life.

Discussion of the Essays

The music box paper (scored 6, superior) exemplifies the excellent writing that some students can produce in forty-five minutes under test conditions. Its wealth of detail, clarity, focus, organization, and amplitude all attest to a student with superior writing skill. "My House" (scored 5, a strong response) is clearly less excellent, but it shows a skillful writer using personification of the house as an original way to fulfill the assignment. Some teachers may be bothered by the relative lack of detail and by the placement of the writer at the center of the essay and so may want to lower the score; others may want to reward even more highly the imaginative quality of the writing. The competent essay, scored 4, reveals a skillful writer undone by a fragmented essay; depending on the program and the institution, this paper might well be placed in the lower half of scores.

We scored "Bear-Bear" at the 3 level (weak response), despite its minimal satisfaction of all requirements of the assignment, on the grounds of its immature approach and stereotyped treatment of the subject. However, the considerable detail and consistent tone argue for a higher score under some circumstances. The generalized paper on cars exemplifies the inadequate (2) essay, which fails to come to grips with the topic and is beset by writing problems, despite a kind of focus and some sentence control. The last essay evinces a student likely to need substantial assistance before succeeding in a regular college composition program.

Although no single test of any type is accurate enough to be used by itself to make irreversible decisions about student programs, the essays presented here suggest possible courses of action. The student who wrote the essay scored 1 (incompetent) might be recommended by this test for remedial or tutorial attention, if further testing and background information support the evaluation. Such a decision might lead to success for a student otherwise heading for failure. At the other end of the spectrum, the student producing the superior (6) essay might be a candidate for credit by examination, if other evidence confirms the ability shown in "The Music Box."

ESSAY SCORING BEYOND THE CLASSROOM: USING GROUP SCORES

If you prepare carefully for a holistic scoring session, selecting sample essays to illustrate the scoring guide and following standard procedures, you and your colleagues should be able to score several hundred essays in a day (with two separate scores for each essay) with about 90 percent agreement within a point on the 6-point scale. Readers can score about twenty-five essays an hour after they have reached general agreement on sample papers in a training session. Although most diagnostic essays are still handled individually by classroom instructors, more and more writing staffs are now accomplishing such group scoring. At the least, it brings the staff together to consider standards; in many cases, it leads to substantial sharing of ideas about the teaching of writing as well as to useful scores for placement. One caution: Unless collegial procedures are followed, respecting differences of opinion, group scoring can backfire and exacerbate existing hostilities.

PRETESTING AND POSTTESTING

One way to try to measure the gains students may have made in writing ability in your course would be to give the placement or diagnostic essay again at the end of the term. The second administration would be the posttest and might show student improvement, if instruction in the course focused on personal-experience writing. (It is a common mistake to use a pretest/posttest assessment without ensuring that what is being tested is in fact what is being taught; if the curriculum asks students to do text-based writing, you should choose topics from Chapter 4 of this book.) You can expect that students will write better, particularly if they have had instruction and practice in that kind of writing.

To ensure that your results are trustworthy, take some precautions against unintentional skewing of the scores. For example, you might save the pretests and grade both pretest and posttest at the same time; further, you could get someone else to cover names and dates and to code the papers so that you would not know whether a particular paper had been written at the beginning or the end of the term. Even more credible would be a system using two different topics. Half of your group could take each topic as a pretest, and each group could write on the other topic at the end of instruction. After coding, you and a colleague or two could grade each question carefully and then compare group pretest scores with posttest scores. Of course, you will want questions that are parallel in their demands on the students (though no two essay questions are ever of exactly the same order of difficulty), and you will have to use identical scoring guides for this purpose.

If you use a system of this sort, you will want to be clear in your mind about the difference between scoring papers for your use (to learn, say, what you have taught most or least successfully) and grading papers for the classification or education of your students. Each of these purposes is legitimate in its own way, but each of them calls for a different approach to grading. For example, if you are grading papers to help students improve their work, you need to supply comments and prepare for discussion that will help students revise subsequent drafts; scoring for a pretest/posttest study requires only highly reliable grades.

USING THE PLACEMENT OR DIAGNOSTIC ESSAY TEST

The essay test based on personal experience has many possible uses: sorting students into appropriate levels of the curriculum, getting the course started in a positive way, teaching planning and revision through an accessible writing topic, developing data for pre-/posttesting and program assessment, and so on. Above all, it demonstrates that writing is what counts in the writing course.

CHAPTER 4

PLACEMENT OR DIAGNOSTIC ESSAY TESTS BASED ON GIVEN TEXTS

---------------- ≪≫ ----------------

This chapter gives two additional diagnostic writing assignments with supporting material (discussion, scoring guides, and sample papers at differing levels of performance). The assignments are based principally on a given text, so the student must begin with examination and explanation of that text. Although some personal experience may well enter the student's response, these topics require much more ability to handle abstract concepts and other people's ideas than the diagnostic essays of Chapter 3. Though each mode of essay has its strengths and problems as a placement or diagnostic test, your particular teaching situation will suggest which is more appropriate for your students.

This book provides pairs of topics in these two chapters so that either kind of topic can serve as a rough pretest or posttest to measure learning outcomes, as described in Chapter 3, as well as a placement or diagnostic writing assignment. If you want or need to do an outcome study, be careful to note that these pairs provide parallel topics, not identical topics and not necessarily topics of identical difficulty, so you will want to use the procedures outlined at the end of Chapter 3 to provide meaningful results. Remember that any pretest/posttest study should use identical scoring guides and topics that in fact measure what your course teaches. Neither of these kinds of topics will tell you anything about library research skills, for instance, or the ability to read poetry. One last tip: If, like most writing instructors, you have little experience at studies derived from social science research techniques, you might want to seek some statistical support for an outcome study from a colleague in psychology, statistics, or education, where such studies are more or less routine.

Whether or not you are engaged in an outcome study, you want to find out as quickly as possible how well your students write. These essay topics are designed, and have been used, as in-class writing assignments for the first day of class. Select one that is appropriate for your class, and it will give you important information you need to be able to teach effectively, as well as allow you to start the writing class with writing.

ESSAY TEST 3: TEXT-BASED TOPIC 1

Many writing courses focus primarily on reading and writing about given texts: essays, literature, or anthologized readings. If your course is text-based and most of your instruction relates to writing about texts, you will probably find a text-based diagnostic essay more appropriate than one based on personal experience. Here is a typical assignment derived from a reading passage:

> The best swordsman in the world doesn't need to fear the second best swords-man in the world; no, the person for him to be afraid of is some ignorant antagonist who has never had a sword in his hand before; he doesn't do the thing he ought to do, and so the expert isn't prepared for him; he does the thing he ought not to do; and often it catches the expert out and ends him on the spot.
>
> —Samuel Clemens

> *Write an essay that explains what Clemens means by his description of the "best swordsman" and the "ignorant antagonist." Relate Clemens's concept to an area about which you are well informed.*

Notice that this assignment makes very different kinds of conceptual demands on the writer than those made by personal-experience topics. Instead of requiring the writer to plumb experience for a person or an object to write about, this question demands close and sensitive reading of the passage as the crucial first step. There is no evidence to show that text-based topics are inherently more difficult than experience-based topics, though they are for some students, or that they elicit more complex thought or writing. All we can say with certainty is that the demands are different and less personal; in some ways, these topics are more "academic" than the first set and will thus have more appeal to faculty across the curriculum, though rather less to most students. The text-based questions in this chapter make complex demands on students in the areas of both reading and writing and so may be more appropriate for advanced students than for those lacking experience with complex texts.

Here is a general scoring guide that is useful for such topics and, in particular, for Essay Test 3.

Holistic Scoring Guide

6. A **superior** response addresses the question fully and explores the issues thoughtfully. It shows substantial depth, fullness, and complexity of thought. The response demonstrates clear, focused, unified, and coherent organization and is fully developed and detailed. The essay evidences superior control of diction, syntactic variety, and transition but may have a few minor flaws.

5. A **strong** response clearly addresses the question and explores the issues. It shows some depth and complexity of thought and is effectively organized. The strong essay is well developed, with supporting detail. It demonstrates control of diction, syntactic variety, and transition, though it may have a few flaws.

4. A **competent** response adequately addresses the question and explores the issues. It shows clarity of thought but may lack complexity. A competent essay is organized and adequately developed, with some detail. This response demonstrates competent writing, though it may have some flaws.

3. A **weak** response may distort or neglect parts of the question. It may be simplistic or stereotyped in thought. It may demonstrate problems in organization. It may use generalizations without supporting detail or detail without generalizations; details may be undeveloped. The weak response shows patterns of error in language, syntax, or mechanics.

2. An **inadequate** response demonstrates serious problems in one or more of the areas specified for the weak (3) response.

1. An **incompetent** response fails in its attempt to discuss the topic, or it may be deliberately off-topic. A response in this category is incompletely developed and mechanically inept.

Sample Student Essays

Score of 6

The Expert Is Always on Guard Against Checkmate

When Clemens speaks of the ''best swordsman,'' he brings up the trained expert, the professional who has mastered the rules of the game. This expert is ready for antagonists who play by the rules. The ''ignorant antagonist'' stands for the untrained or rebellious outsider who reserves the right to make up his own rules. The opposition between these two ways of fighting, playing, or living applies in many different ways.

When revolutionaries break diplomatic rules by engaging in acts of terrorism, the governments affected are often ''caught out'' and government leaders sometimes ''ended on the spot.'' In today's world, the superpowers ready their defense for major confrontations with other superpowers or ''second best'' powers, but not for isolated and unpredictable acts of terrorism such as the taking of hostages, the assassination of political figures, or the hijacking of a plane—often for personal or even crazy reasons.

On the other hand, unconventional chess players don't have the slightest chance against an expert unless these outsiders are well beyond the novice stage. The brilliant innovations in chess have nothing to do with ignorance. No expert can lose to the novice opening with rook pawns or carelessly throwing his queen into opening positions. A brilliant amateur can win at chess, where nothing can by this time be entirely new, but the innovator cannot be ignorant. However, chess is here, as elsewhere, atypical. What Clemens says does not apply in this tight, square world, so unlike the disorderly real one.

Any proverb has a basic truth but needs to be applied with care. Maybe the very best experts are those most alert to the ways unconventional moves can work. Our swordsmen in foreign relations need to be ready for mobs, terrorists, and others who will refuse to acknowledge our rules. If the ignorant antagonist can do in the duelist, the swordsman has more to learn.

Score of 5

Uncle Fred

The Clemens passage reminds me of a saying heard often in our family: ''You can't argue with an ignorant man.'' This line has been repeated whenever someone mentions my Uncle Fred. Fred plays the part of the ''ignorant antagonist'' on many subjects, but most especially in politics and religion.

Although Clemens speaks metaphorically, Uncle Fred is a literal example as well. A genuine ''ignorant antagonist,'' he never takes the time to become informed on any one political, party, candidate, or issue. He hears bits and pieces of news stories and reads headlines and political cartoons in his local small-town newspaper and then forms his opinions.

When Fred claims that the Russian leaders will always take advantage of the Americans, because they are so much smarter, we have learned not to argue. In the next breath, Fred might say, ''I think Yeltsin has been sent to save the world. He is going to achieve world peace.'' The next day Fred declares, ''Congress is so stupid, they let the state department manipulate them on everything.'' First, our government is not smart enough to protect us from Yeltsin, then Yeltsin is going to save us. Finally, the state department is too smart for 435 elected representatives, despite its stupidity. It isn't that Fred has a blind loyalty to any one party or that he is against all of them. He just changes his opinions as quickly as the stories change on the news broadcasts.

You can't argue with a man like Fred, just as the ''best swordsman in the world'' can't fence with the ''ignorant antagonist who has never had a sword in his hand before,'' because he doesn't play by recognized rules. He changes the rules as he goes along. This can in part be explained by using Berne's Transactional Analysis theory. When an adult interacts with another person, he anticipates how the other person will respond. Things usually go smoothly when the person responds correctly, that is, according to the unstated rules of adult transactions. However, if the person responds using an unanticipated ego state (say, child instead of adult, or parent instead of child), you get a crossed transaction, which often ''catches the expert out and ends him on the spot.''

Score of 4

The Best Soldier

The best soldier in the world does not fear the second best soldier of any country. The soldier that he must respect and fear is the nonprofessional soldier. the one who has no set standard of fighting or long regimental traditions. The ''ignorant antagonist'' as he relates to me is untrained and unskilled in the latest military arts. These people have never held a rifle in their hands with the intent of killing another human being.

The unconventional soldier does not use the usual military tactics that the best soldier uses. His is the world of the underground. The expert is not prepared for this opponent.

The ''ignorant antagonist'' in the low intensaty conflict is the soldier of his/her land. They fight a war that is unconventional and usually very deadly to the best soldier. Throughout history there are examples of such fighters besting the best soldiers. Our American Revolution is a good example of ''ignorant antagonists'' beating an army that was considered the best. The lines of redcoats were no match for the farmers that used what we call today cover and concealment to engage the on comming best soldiers.

The minute men, as they were called, blended in well with nature and destroyed the will of the best soldiers to continue the fight. Recently, the Afghan rebels gave the best Russian soldiers a run for their money. In Central America the contras are making it difficult for the Marxist government to expand their hold on the country. The Sandanistas are the best soldiers in that region of the world.

The ''ignorant antagonist'' usually has the best chance of winning the contest if the fight is short. But there is one difference that the antagonist might overlook, and that will be his undoing and the expert will ''catch *him* out and end him on the spot.'' That difference is flexibility. What made the expert the best in the first place was the ability to reason, to understand that his way has been time proven through many trials, to adapt, to learn new ways. At that point, the roles are reversed, for the best becomes the ''ignorant antagonist'' and the ignorant antagonist becomes the best. Thus you have a situation that the ''ignorant antagonist'' does make mistakes and that buys time for the ''best swordsman'' to counter his blows.

The one who makes the least mistakes wins the contest. It takes 50,000 dead and wounded soldiers to train a general. Can the ''ignorant antagonist'' pay that price? I believe he can and does. The best wins the battle with no dead and wounded, but that is not the rule but the exception. The best must be aware and fear the ignorant for the ignorant do not know what to fear about the best.

Score of 3

The Better Man Doesn't Always Win

Samuel Clemens story about the best swordsman can best be related to that old cliché: ''The better man doesn't always win.''

Clemens story about the best swordsman best depicts a situation that I have experienced in basketball. My situation deals with a basketball game I was playing in, when I was in High School. When I was in High School, I thought of myself as being a fairly good basketball player. This feeling soon changed when I was matched up against a person who I felt I was better than. This person was terrible in the game of basketball. This individual couldn't dribble, shoot, or even walk for that matter. But, there was one thing he could do very well, and that was gaurd me. Like the antagonist in the best swordsman, this individual was awful. His defensive play was like none I had ever seen before, it was awkward and unorthodox. This individual was so bad that after a quarter of play, he made me look bad. I couldn't understand it, every move I used to fake him out wouldn't work. Every time I would put a move on him to get past him, he would be right there to stop me. After a quarter of this, I became frustrated and got benched, much like the best swordsman's end.

In conclusion, I feel this story about the best swordsman best depicts my situation. In my situation, the awful defensive man is much like the antagonist in the best swordsman. In that, like the swordsman, anything I did to the

antagonist to beat him, wouldn't work. Consequently, I was
sent to the bench, much like the best swordsman was put to his
end.

Score of 2

Freshman Coach

The passage by Samuel Clemens reminds me of a Junior
College basketball coach, and his Freshman athletes. Here,
like the ''best swordsman,'' is the Coach: a man who knows his
craft but fears the ignorant antagonist; the Freshman
athletes. Why? because the basic skills of dribbling,
passing, rebounding and shooting that his Freshman athletes
should of learned in High School; the majority of these
Freshman athletes don't possess. Because practice time to
teach those skills one on one is short, this puts fears in the
coach who feels these Freshman athletes should already be
prepared.

By lacking these skills the Freshman athletes, like the
ignorant antagonist dosen't do what the coach expects from
him, because the Freshman figure they already know from their
previous basketball experience what to do.

Because the Freshman athletes have their own
preconceived notions that their prepared with these skills,
this makes the Coach who is the expert feel not prepared. The
Coach now feels like he must start all over teaching the basic
skills to young adults who should have learned these skills
from their adolescence to teen-age lives.

This passage shows us how the best ''the Coach,'' can be fearful of the ignorant antagonist ''the Freshman athletes,'' because when the Coach is not prepared for the ignorant antagonist ''the Freshman athletes'' he finds himself pushed to be the best.

Score of 1

The Best the Stronger

The passage tells us about the best swordsman, and the first thing we find it to know who is the ''best swordsman,'' but this would be different from genration to genration, and from surroundings to surrounding. The swordsman usually like to fight, like to tell the people around him, he is the stronger. In the other hand the ignorant antagonist does not like to fight and has never had a sword in his hand. Why he never had sword, because he hate to be enemy to be agrassion. The swordsman often does not know Clemens's concepts. He hate the people and fight them maybe because he is not want to see any body more healthy or welthy than him. In my home country I know, both the swordsman and the ignorant antagonist. Therefore some of swordsman different than other depends where is he live what kind of his invironment, some of the people who leave in desert, and mountain area. Those are often agressive, and like to fight the people with reason and with out reason. I think the motive for the that only to be the best the stronger the first man, but some of them to struggle to sarvive. The swordsman with the new life became

less enemy than before. They became to have Clemens and let
the people to live. The ignorant antagonist those people in
the area which I live in had never had sword to kill the
people or to make anything for the people. Those persons like
the people to have good life with out any problem with out
fighting let the people to have wonderful time in their life.
They know exactly what Clemens means, and why it's important
for the people and for their life. The swordsman should be
live, and let the people to live. They should go around him
and see what the people do, and do as the people. The
compassion is very important to compassinate the children
and the elderly people. This is the life, and this is the good
way in this life.

Discussion of the Essays

The superior response (scored 6) exemplifies the description in the scoring
guide. The writer begins by defining terms, accomplishing the task of explaining
what Clemens means by using terms that can be applied "in many different
ways." For this writer, the opposition between the "trained expert" and the
"rebellious outsider" works in foreign relations—and the writer shows just
how—but does not work in the "tight, square world" of chess, "so unlike the
disorderly real one." Though the response is necessarily brief, given the time
limit, the writer does explain the meaning and apply it in two other areas;
throughout, the writer is clearly thinking about meanings and applications.
The demonstration that the quotation works on some occasions but not on
others shows complexity of thought, and the tight focus of the essay shows
careful organization. The essay includes such details as the taking of hostages
and chess openings with rook pawns. Finally, the writer shows accomplished
control of style, diction, and other aspects of writing.

   The essay on Uncle Fred was scored 5, even though the discussion of the
quotation appears only in the last paragraph. This writer began immediately
with Uncle Fred, as a way of exploring the meanings of the quotation, using

dialogue and detail; the writer sees Uncle Fred as the "ignorant antagonist" that no expert can handle. The paper is focused and responsive to the question, though it lacks the depth and writing skill of the 6 paper.

"The Best Soldier" opens with four strong paragraphs connecting the quotation to military history, using details from a series of wars to exemplify the meaning. Unfortunately, the last two paragraphs wander off the subject and do not seem to connect with either what has come before or the quotation. Nonetheless, the strength of the first four paragraphs shows the competence of the writer and justifies the score of 4.

The essay scored 3 (weak response) reflects a common mistake in approaching essay tests. Instead of attending to the meaning of the text, this writer glanced at it and moved to a personal-experience narrative. But unlike "Uncle Fred," the experience here seems vague, lacking in detail, and not altogether related to the quotation. The opposing basketball player, we are told, was "terrible" but nonetheless succeeded in outplaying the writer with unorthodox moves. Most readers were unconvinced by this essay because the assertions that the opposing player was an ignorant antagonist are contradicted by his success, and the writer presents himself as anything but expert. The writer clearly knows how to proceed, but the unsupported generalizations and simplistic view of the quotation move the paper into the lower half of scores.

Nonetheless, the weak response shows an understanding of the passage that the inadequate response (scored 2) does not reach. Here we are told about the coach and the unwilling freshman, but the meaning of the quotation is lost. In addition, the problems with sentence structure indicate a weak writer who may, depending on the institution, profit from special tutorial or developmental instruction before or during a composition class. Finally, the incompetent response (scored 1) betrays severe problems with reading comprehension and language use, probably a sign of inadequate skill in English as a second language. Without special support services of some kind, this student will not be able to succeed in freshman-level work in college.

ESSAY TEST 4: TEXT-BASED TOPIC 2

The following assignment differs somewhat from the previous one by using two quotations and requiring a comparison-and-contrast response. If you are using it with the first text-based topic, in a pretest/posttest study, you should probably use only the first quotation (which works well by itself) and prepare directions for writing that are parallel to those for the Clemens passage. In addition, you should use exactly the same scoring guide, revised appropriately for the abilities of your students and for the specific skills taught in your course. I present the question as an example of a difficult essay assignment with complex demands.

This question requires that students (1) understand two passages, both of which are metaphorical and in part ironic; (2) recognize the attitude each passage reflects toward the role of science in human affairs; (3) conceive and present an imaginary argument between the protagonist of one passage (the scientist) and the deceived "some" who speak in the other; (4) speculate on the views of the authors of the two passages; and (5) organize and present this material in an orderly and literate way under time pressure. Clearly, such an assignment requires substantial academic preparation. If you have many students such as those scoring in the lower ranges on Essay Test 3, this question will not yield useful information for diagnosis or anything else. But this assignment, or one with even more extensive reading passages, may be just what you need if you are teaching students who have had the benefit of rigorous academic preparation.

Read the passage and the poem; then write an essay as directed following the poem.

This is a story about one of our great atomic physicists. This man, one of the chief architects of the atomic bomb, so the story runs, was out wandering in the woods one day with a friend when he came upon a small tortoise. Overcome with pleasurable excitement, he took up the tortoise and started home, thinking to surprise his children with it. After a few steps he paused and surveyed the tortoise doubtfully.

"What's the matter?" asked his friend.

Without responding, the great scientist slowly retraced his steps as precisely as possible, and gently set the turtle down upon the exact spot from which he had taken him up.

Then he turned solemnly to his friend. "It just struck me," he said, "that perhaps, for one man, I have tampered enough with the universe." He turned, and left the turtle to wander on its way.

—Loren Eiseley

"The path of life," some say, "is hard and rough
Only because we do not know enough.

> When Science has discovered something more,
> We shall be happier than we were before."
>   —Hilaire Belloc

Explain each writer's attitude toward the relationship between science and human happiness.

To what extent do the scientist in Eiseley's passage and the "some" in Belloc's poem agree or disagree?

Do the two authors seem to agree more with the scientist or with the "some"?

Holistic Scoring Guide

6. Superior responses will be well-organized essays that address the three parts of the assignment. They will accurately explain each author's attitude, discussing directly or implicitly the irony in the poem, showing where the two selections are similar and how they differ, and indicating how the authors seem to agree more with the scientist than with the "some." Generalizations will be supported with appropriate details. The superior essay will display a high degree of competence generally but may have slight flaws in writing, consistent with timed, first-draft prose.

5. Strong essays will address all parts of the assignment, display good overall interpretations of both selections, and clearly demonstrate strong reading and writing, but they may be less fluent or thoroughly developed than the superior papers, may reveal some inaccuracy in interpretation, or may contain minor grammatical errors or occasional awkwardness.

4. Competent essays will adequately address all parts of the question but may lack the development of higher-scoring responses, may perceive similarities and differences somewhat less accurately, or may contain some errors in sentence construction or usage. They may deal with one aspect of the assignment by implication rather than by direct statement.

3. Weak essays may show signs of strong writing but respond to only one or two parts of the assignment, may contain misinterpretations of both selections or a radical misinterpretation of one, may show evidence of serious deficiencies in writing, or may lack sufficient details to support their generalizations.

2. Inadequate responses may show serious problems in reading and understanding the selections, reveal serious patterns of faults in writing, display considerable irrelevance, or be simplistic.

1. Incompetent essays will reflect almost no understanding of the question or the selections, and the writing will display ineptness in sentence construction, usage, and idiom.

Sample Student Essays

Score of 6

Science Is No Panacea

In the first passage, the writer is illustrating by the anecdote that science is not necessarily a good or beneficial thing to human beings. The inventor of the atom bomb seems somewhat regretful that he used his scientific knowledge to invent something so destructive to people and the earth. This regret is illustrated by his reluctance to tamper with even the simplest laws of nature; that is, the progress of the turtle in the woods.

The second passage takes a more ironic, mocking tone. It is saying essentially the same thing as the first, even though it looks different, by using a poem and the phrase, ''some say.'' Who are ''some''? The author makes us doubt seriously the quote from the ''some'' by deliberately leaving it vague. All we know is that they have a blind belief in the virtues of science: ''When Science has discovered something more, we shall be happier than before.'' This is very insubstantial and illogical. It does not follow that science will change life from being ''hard and rough'' to something better; maybe (as with the Industrial Revolution) many people will be even worse off.

The ''some'' in the second passage don't agree with the scientist in the first. The ''some'' have no scientific knowledge; just a hazy idea that more scientific discoveries will make life easier. The scientist knows that this is not necessarily so because he has ample facts on which to base his knowledge. The development of the atomic bomb did not make life easier or less rough. In fact for a lot of people in Hiroshima there was no more life, period, because of this ''scientific discovery.'' The ''some'' in the poem have no specific data to back up their claim—it is a generalized statement based on lack of specific knowledge of anything scientific.

The two authors seem to agree more with the scientist than with the ''some.'' The scientist in the first passage has found out what the ''some'' in the second passage still don't know. Science needs to be handled with care; all scientific progress, discoveries, and work do not necessarily lead to health, wealth, and happiness. The ''some'' in the second passage are truly ignorant of this, and they are probably the very people who pay for scientists to work on anything bigger or more advanced in the hope that it will bring them ''true'' happiness.

The author of the second passage, by spotlighting this glaring ignorance, is mocking the ''some,'' and is in agreement with the first author that science is not the panacea for all human ills.

Score of 5

Fear of Science

Throughout history, people have debated the usefulness of science for the betterment of human life. Sometimes research threatened religion, and religious leaders raised voices in protest; sometimes scientific remedies were viewed as the path to human salvation.

These passages from Eiseley and Belloc illustrate the logical fear of the human hand interfering with nature. Eiseley relates a story, almost a parable, about a designer of the world's most devastating weapon, the atomic bomb. This physicist was overcome with joy at finding a tortoise to bring home to his children. But some small respect for nature or a pervasive guilt from creating the atom bomb causes him to put the creature back, as near to where he found it as possible because he fears that he has tampered with the universe enough for one man.

Of course, his major ''tampering'' has already been accomplished by the time he discovers his conscience. Eiseley is illustrating the human burden of responsibility that comes with scientific experimentation.

One doesn't know the effect that an invention can have on fellow human beings.

Invention of the machine did give leisure time to many, but also damned others to a life of drudgery and boredom, destroyed eardrums, and bad backs. Creation of mechanized factories caused city crowding, which led to crimes, pollution, and other urban problems.

Belloc, in capitalizing ''Science,'' seems to banish the idea that ''Science will bring happiness'' to the realm of myth. The rhyme, simplistic and childlike, makes those who espouse this belief seem silly.

Belloc's ''some,'' trusting and naive, rely on the wisdom of scientists, not realizing that they are human, prone to act on ego or for other human but less than humanitarian reasons. They equate intelligence and knowledge with wisdom, not realizing that scientists (or ''Science''—''The Force'') can have regrets like Eiseley's scientist coping with his guilt in a token way.

Both authors seem to agree with the scientist that humans must be cautious in their tampering and must think of all of the possible effects of what they are creating.

Score of 4

Science Makes Things Worse

In the passages, Eiseley and Belloc seem to agree in most areas. It is my belief that Belloc's passage is written with sarcasm and that this is the factor which tends to unite the meanings of the two passages. I feel that both Eiseley and Belloc believe that science is ultimately destructive although it may seem to be a way to positive progress.

The final decision of the scientist, in Eiseley's passage to leave the turtle in its natural surroundings shows symbolically that the world should not be tampered with. Also, Eiseley demonstrates in his passage that the scientist has some regrets for creating something as destructive as the atomic bomb. I feel these are expressions of Eiseley's personal opinion on the subject of science and its negative effects upon nature.

I feel that Belloc, also, would agree that the scientist made the proper decision by letting the turtle remain in the woods. My reason for this opinion is that Belloc's use of the word ''some'' is outright sarcasm and is used to represent others besides himself. Yet another example of Belloc's sarcasm is the part of the passage which says happiness comes from scientific discovery. Illustrating how far-fetched this idea is, the scientist in Eiseley's passage was not happy after his discovery of the atomic bomb but, instead, he was regretful.

Although scientific innovation seems to be a synonym for progress, I find myself forced to agree with Eiseley and Belloc. To me, science only tampers with nature in such a way as to worsen our natural conditions. Belloc and Eiseley, I'm sure, would be proud to here me state such an opinion.

Score of 3

Science and Human Happiness

Loren Eisely and Hilaire Belloc express different views toward the relationship between science and human happiness. Their attitudes voice the contravercy between the need for the knowledge which science offers and it's conscious limitation to avoid the possible destructive ends it sometimes promotes, such as the atomic bomb mentioned in Eiselely's passage. The extent to which the scientist in

Eiseley's passage and the ''some'' in Belloc's passage agree
or disagree is the manifestation of this contravercy.

In Loren Eiseley's passage their is a very concerned
attitude expressed toward the relationship between science
and human happiness. Eiseley views science as being
destructive to human happiness through it's creation of
atomic warfare. His protagonast replaces a turtle to it's
natural habitat in a symbolic gesture of not further
''tampering with the universe'' as he had previously done as
one of the architects of the atomic bomb. Eiseley obviously
believes that science can go beyond a reasonable limit, that
it can and has been a destructive force in human happiness.
The very least which it has done is to cause one man
(Eiseley's protagonist) to question the morality of
tampering with the universe in any way, even such an
apparantly insignificant act as removing a tortoise from the
wild. Eiseley's expressing through his protagonast his
concern for the need to restrict the tampering with the
universe and thus with human happiness. Science has the power
to do this.

Hilaire Belloc expresses a somewhat different view of
science than does Eiseley. Belloc observes the hardships in
life and their relationship to ignorance. Science is
knowledge; it discovers new things which conquor the
ignorance and thus the hardships in human life. He places his
foundation on the relationship between happiness and
hardships, deducing that a decrease in hardships will
produce an increase in human happiness. The validity of this

foundation may be questionable, but Belloc uses it as a
premise to indirectly saying that science has a direct
bearing on human happiness. We need science, science will
make us happier by removing our hardships. This is a very
different view than Loren Eiseley's.

    The extent to which the scientist in Eiseley's passage
and the ''some'' in Belloc's agree or dissagree is the voicing
of the contravercy between the need to promote or to limit
science. The scientist and the ''some'' are not in agreement.
Eiseley's scientist feels that science interferes with the
univers, that it tampers with things which should be left
alone. His tortoise is a very symbolic representative of
this. Belloc's ''some'' feel that science promotes knowledge
and ends hardship, thus helping people in their strive for
happiness. This is a complete disagreement; a contravercy
between the limits and morality of science.

    Both Loren Eiseley and Hilaire Belloc side with their
protagonasts in their views concerning the necessary
limitations of science. The argument between the scientist
and the ''some'' is the same as between Eiseley and Belloc,
both presenting different views on the limits and morality of
science.

Score of 2

Different Attitudes

    Attitudes of Loren Eiseley and Hilaire Belloc toward
the relationship between scince and human happiness are
different in the following way.

Loren Eiseley, in his passage about one of our great atomic physisists, shows that this man who challenged nature in the most vialent way by taking the atomic power from it still thinks that there are some things that a man should not touch in order to be happy. This is described in the scientists's words when he was walking in the woods with his friend and picked up a tortoise but put it back after giving it some thought: ''. . . perhaps, for one man, I have tempered enough with the universe.''

Hilaire Belloc, however, describes in his passage about what ''some'' say about science a significantly different attitude. ''Some'' say that ''. . . life is hard and rough only because we don't know enough'' and that scientists should temper with nature as much as possible and that ''when science has discovered something more, we shall be happier than before.''

Score of 1

Agreement on Science

When the great atomic physicists saw the tortoise he was full of excitement. He had thought he could have had fun with it at home with his family. As soon as the tortoise stuck him he realized that it would be happier if it was left to wander its own way. Belloc says ''We say the path to life is hard and rough only because we don't know.'' Personally I think Eiseley and Belloc agree to the fact that there is a lot of things we don't know, thus we say its rough or hard simply because we don't know. Sooner or later when things get

discovered and we start knowing things life will be easier
and we will be happier than before.

Both of the authors seem to agree on science. Eiseley
feels that he has already tampered anough with the universe
and doesn't feel like dealing with the tortoise. He'd rather
leave it alone and let it wander whereas Belloc feels that
it's only because enough things haven't been discovered so as
to let us know what will make us happy or what is good from
what is bad. In a way I agree with what Belloc says because
the more things are discovered through science or tecnology
the happier humans are because life gets to be easier and we
wouldn't have to be wandering all the time. A solution or
conclusion has been reached. The passage and the poem
disagree at the point where the physicists chooses to let the
tortoise wander the way it wishes to and Belloc says it's only
because it doesn't know what is good or bad for it. The
tortoise could be happy under the physicists care than it
would be just out in the woods. So more discoveris have to be
done to make even the animals as happy as humans. It seems
like both authors look at human rights scientifically and
logically according to the way they feel or they define human
rights in relation with science.

Discussion of the Essays

Both the superior (6) and the strong (5) essays demonstrate careful and
incisive readings of the two selections, answering all parts of the question
and showing good control of organization, diction, and mechanics. The
major distinction is in the depth of the 6 paper's reading of Belloc. These

papers show extraordinary ability to handle a complex reading and writing job under time pressure.

The competent (4) essay also answers all parts of the question and understands the reading, but at a comparatively superficial and undeveloped level. Shadings of meaning that the better responses describe pass this writer by; for example, whereas the 6 essay notes Belloc's "more ironic, mocking tone," and the 5 essay points out that Belloc's "some" are "trusting and naive" and his rhymes are "simplistic and childlike," the 4 essay sees only "outright sarcasm." Nonetheless, this paper accomplishes the task adequately and with clarity.

Despite poor spelling, the weak (3) essay recognizes that the issue of the comparison/contrast has to do with the values, limitations, and dangers of science. It presents a clear reading of the Eiseley passage. But, in common with the other lower-rated (3, 2, or 1) work, the Belloc poem, with its ironies, poses unsolvable problems for this writer. The essay shows that the test is to a large degree a reading examination, for without the sophisticated reading skills that give access to the Belloc poem, no writer can handle this question.

The inadequate response (2) summarizes the Eiseley passage with limited accuracy and then quotes several chunks of the poem. But the question goes largely unanswered, and its separate sections are ignored. It is better than the 1 paper, for it goes through the motions of comparison and contrast, but all it does is assert that the selections have "a significantly different attitude" without explaining what that difference is or what it means.

The incompetent (1) response demonstrates only the dimmest awareness of the meanings of the selections, with writing that seems to go in a variety of directions at once.

CONSTRUCTIVE NOTES ON ESSAY TESTS

You will notice some common characteristics among the essay topics given in this chapter and Chapter 3. Each of them has been developed for a testing program; that is, each has been refined over a long period of time to make sure that it works as an essay test question. Essay test developers conclude that a question works if (1) it is clear enough in its demands so that graders can tell if the question has been answered or not and can thus score the papers consistently, (2) it leads to a range of scores that truly reflect the range of abilities in the group (instead of clumping scores in the middle, as many questions do), (3) it allows all students in the test group to write something and is interesting enough to stimulate genuine responses, and (4) it is free of bias and does not place any group members at an advantage or a disadvantage.

Sometimes teachers are tempted to use very general or vague questions ("discuss") in the belief that such lack of clarity will allow students more range in formulating answers. And sometimes teachers will ask questions on emotional topics or "hot" topics from the day's news, in the expectation that such questions will elicit better writing. But experienced test writers avoid such questions, just as they avoid questions that offer the religious an opportunity to recite their beliefs: Such topics usually lead even the best students to trot out undemonstrated or half-digested clichés that teachers find impossible to grade consistently or to respond to sympathetically.

The underlying role of essay test questions such as those I have supplied is to help students see that there are real differences between papers of high and low quality; students are much more apt to revise their work (as are professional writers) when they themselves can see what needs to be improved. Thus the scoring guides and sample essays have an important teaching function: They can help students learn to evaluate their own writing and to see what they must do to make it better.

At the same time, teachers and administrators need to be cautious in interpreting the results of essay tests, even precise and clear ones that have been shown to work. Students can perform badly on an essay test for a wide variety of reasons, from a headache to lack of preparation for a specialized task (such as the reading of ironic poetry such as Belloc's). In particular, students for whom English is not a first language are likely to require time for revision and editing that is not usually allowed on essay tests.

First-draft writing *is* a form of writing, and it may have a strong correlation to writing done under less pressured circumstances, so it is surely worth examining. Further, it does provide a useful way to show students important differences between successful and less successful work. But one test score is best interpreted in a limited way: The student wrote in a certain way on the particular question at a particular time under test conditions. The score suggests certain abilities that may or may not show up under other conditions. It is unwise and unprofessional to generalize about a student's abilities on the basis of one test score, without other evidence. But that score may draw the attention of faculty to students who need help if they are to succeed in college.

CHAPTER 5

EXIT AND PROFICIENCY ASSESSMENTS

This chapter focuses on two kinds of institutional writing assessments that often occur on campus:

- Exit assessments for multisection courses, which may determine or affect students' final grades

- Proficiency barrier assessments at the sophomore ("rising junior") level or at the upper-division level, which may determine whether or not a student will be allowed to continue toward the degree or graduate

Although these assessments differ, certain general principles of writing assessment apply in both cases. Because these are institutional rather than classroom assessments, we are usually involved with committees that represent a variety of views; we cannot merely act in accordance with what we think is right but must convince the committee to follow those principles. Because writing faculty are usually asked to participate in or even coordinate these assessments, this chapter is designed to assist faculty in applying those principles in a situation many of them find awkward or repellent. As many faculty have discovered to their surprise, each of these assessments is much more complicated than it appears to be, so complex that instructors some-times feel that testing professionals or other administrators should handle all the details. Yet the effects of the assessments are profound for students, teach-ers, and the curriculum; writing teachers must be present, informed, and vocal when decisions are made, or else crucial matters slip away from the faculty and into the hands of administrators and clerks who may know noth-ing about the teaching of writing. I urge writing teachers on campuses with assessment programs to insist on playing a role in them. The following discus-sion only suggests issues and procedures for faculty; the works in the short bibliography at the end of the chapter will provide much more detailed infor-mation.

PROCEDURES FOR DEVELOPING ASSESSMENTS

An assessment is, in one sense, a means of gathering information. This suggests that we should be clear about what information we want and how we will use it before we decide about the means of gathering it. Another way to conceptual-ize the issue is to think of an assessment as providing answers to questions; the questions need to be well formulated before we seek the answers. These ways of thinking about any assessment seem natural enough, but few assessment programs actually follow them. In most cases, the method of assessment is the first issue decided instead of the last; the answer is sought before the question has become clear. Typically, some influential campus figure or group presses for a particular test (often measures published and heavily promoted by some testing firm) or a new type of assessment (such as portfolios) as a valuable device in itself. But it is wasteful and intrusive to gather more information than we can use, and it is unconscionable to use instructional funds to gather information that has no instructional purpose. Furthermore, it is dishonest to use a test designed for one purpose (college admission, for example) as if it provided information for another (writing placement), even if the data are already on hand. Before we decide on any assessment method, we must insist that it respond to clearly articulated goals.

This means that the first job of developing a writing assessment is to establish not only its purpose but also just what information is needed to accomplish that purpose. And as faculty we should also consider—and require that the committee consider—how the assessment will affect the students and the programs being assessed. Only after those decisions have been made does it make sense to choose a particular assessment instrument. For example, if we want evidence about the improvement of student writing that occurs as a result of a year's work in freshman composition, we cannot just choose one of the many commercially available multiple-choice tests that purport to give scores for "writing." We need first to ascertain just what has been taught in that writing course, consider how it may reasonably be measured, and keep in mind how our decision on an assessment device might ultimately affect the course. Again, if the course has focused on development of argument and evidence, use of the library, and discovery of individual voice, we need to find ways of measuring those matters.

We also need to balance the expense of assessments in time and money against the information we need. Most writing instructors are partial to portfolio assessments these days and so are likely to argue that portfolios should be used for any writing assessment. But if all that is needed is, say, a pass/fail decision based on sentence and paragraph construction, a short essay test may provide that information at a small fraction of the cost of a portfolio assessment.

Most commercial tests for the purposes we are considering will fail to measure what campus committees regard as most important. It is unlikely that the general criteria for a commercial test will fit the particular needs of a local assessment, that the usual multiple-choice format of those tests will be able to measure the active generation of text that most writing programs teach, or that the norm group used by the commercial test firm to establish the meaning of scores will match the local population. The temptation to accept a commercial test that claims to measure what the campus is looking for is hard to resist, as it is both convenient and cheap to adopt an existing measure. But no matter how economical such a choice may appear to be, it can become extremely costly when the information it produces is not the information needed.

In almost all cases, campus committees will have to follow a series of steps to develop assessment goals, specifications, and criteria. Not until these matters have been decided is it time to ask about the kind of assessment that may deliver what is needed.

Sometimes assessment goals are clear and straightforward: Which students write well enough to pass freshman composition? At other times, the goals are complicated and political: Which students write so badly that they should not receive a college degree despite passing grades in their courses? But every assessment program needs stated, preferably written goals, for everything that follows depends on them. For example, one placement testing program set out its goals as follows: (1) Identify students lacking the sentence construction and readings skills required for entry into freshman composition; (2) deliver support services to these students before entry into the first-year class, increasing their passing rate in freshman composition by at least 50 percent; and (3) upgrade the freshman composition curriculum by removing elementary sentence and reading skills and replacing them with a new focus on developing and supporting ideas. The interweaving of assessment and curriculum goals in this series is typical of goals developed with heavy faculty participation.

Once the goals have been clarified, assessment specifications can follow. If a goal is to discover which students write well enough to pass freshman composition at the end of the course, the specifications will list just what is required to do so—for example, "Students must provide evidence of ability to integrate library research into an expository essay" or "Students must be able to produce on demand a coherent and developed essay responding to a given text." The specifications for a course exit exam normally emerge from the course syllabus, and they usually require a series of faculty meetings to reach consensus on what is or should be going on in class. By contrast, specifications for a more general goal (such as to discover which students write well enough to receive the college degree) may call for a much broader consensus by the entire college community. The specifications cannot be so general that they lack real meaning ("Students should write at the college level"); they must be precise enough to lead to an assessment device.

Once the assessment specifications have been made clear, decisions must be reached on the criteria for their measurement. What level or levels of performance will the assessment seek to determine? Is the assessment to judge minimal competency (however that may be defined) and thus focus on a failing cut score? Or is it to reward the topmost group and thus pay the most attention to definitions of excellence? What criteria will allow a university to assert that only competent writers are receiving the bachelor's degree? In some cases, the criteria can be set only tentatively, to await the results of the actual assessment; the performance of real people on an assessment often surprises its designers.

EXIT EXAMINATIONS

Course exit assessments may occur in any large multisection course, but our principal concern here will be the most typical example, freshman composition. On many campuses, students must achieve a particular level on the exit examination in order to pass the course, whatever the judgment of the class instructor may be. A more flexible version of the exit assessment is the coursewide assessment that is advisory: The class instructor must take the student's score into account (perhaps as some specified percentage of the final grade), but the instructor is ultimately responsible for that grade. In all cases, the exit examination attempts to mandate coursewide standards for classes that may be taught by as many as a hundred different instructors.

There are strong arguments for exit assessments, particularly when the teachers are relative beginners or graduate students. The assessment, which may be a test, an exchange of papers among instructors, a portfolio review, or some variety or combination of measures, requires that instructors agree on common goals, specifications, and criteria for the course. Though no one would expect perfect uniformity from section to section, and though considerable latitude in reaching the goals is customary, students are entitled to approximately the same kinds of requirements and standards whatever section they may be in. The examination not only encourages this communality but also fosters continuing discussion of the curriculum and ways of teaching. Finally, the exit examination establishes a kind of credibility for the course for the administration, the faculty, and even the students.

There are also strong arguments against such examinations, particularly where the number of sections is relatively small and where the faculty are more experienced. Most experienced faculty resent any outsiders evaluating their students, believing that their repeated experiences with students' writing and individual conferences give them a better basis for fair judgment than any single assessment. Where there is a wide variety of course goals, reading assignments, and philosophies of instruction, no assessment will please everybody, nor will any compromise satisfy all. If the exit examination is perceived by the instructors as a mandated supervisory function by the administration (instead of as a collegial exercise under their own control that supports teaching), they are likely to dislike and undermine it.

A campus that can use the advantages of an exit examination while avoiding its disadvantages has much to gain. A faculty member and a committee asked to develop such an examination have a delicate balancing act to perform, calling for wide consultation on goals and criteria as well as broad participation in the assessment.

After the goals, specifications, and criteria have been discussed and a reasonable consensus has been achieved, it is time to consider the assessment instrument. In most cases, the choice will be between an essay test and a portfolio assessment (a multiple-choice test contradicts the very notion of writing performance). In making that choice, practical and theoretical concepts collide, with portfolios theoretically more satisfying but essays more practical.

The advantages of an essay test for exit examination are clear. One can be developed that examines many of the specifications for freshman composition, the test can be managed efficiently and relatively inexpensively, and the scores generated by such a test correlate highly with other writing performance for many students. Without much trouble, data can be developed that demonstrate validity and reliability, and the test has high credibility with the rest of the faculty.

But the disadvantages of an essay test are also clear. Most obviously, it usually asks only for first-draft writing, whereas many writing courses insist on revision as essential to the writing process. The test also necessarily restricts writing to at most two kinds, which are assumed to stand for all the writing in the course. Further, it defines writing as test writing to external demands, a partial definition offensive to educators with more romantic views of the expressive and cognitive possibilities that writing can offer students.

A portfolio assessment can preclude most of these essay test objections but presents special problems of its own, which I detail in Chapter 7. Even the exemplary portfolio assessment at the State University of New York at Stony Brook, which launched portfolio assessment in writing, has lately run into difficulties (see Pat Belanoff and Marcia Dickson, *Portfolios: Process and Product*, Portsmouth, NH: Boynton/Cook, 1991).

It is important to keep in mind that any assessment will deliver flawed and compromised information; enormous expenditures of time and money can give the most accurate data, but faculty will properly resist such expense at the cost of instruction. We might well adopt the "good enough" notion from sociology, where some scholars argue that superparenting is not a family requirement; "good enough" parenting yields about the same results. An exit exam needs to be good enough to bring the faculty together on goals and standards but not so good as to interfere with the creativity or individual teaching styles of teachers. The scores yielded by such an assessment ought to be good enough to be useful to teachers grading their students but not so good as to determine student grades all by themselves.

We should resist the simplification that values the results of a single exam or of a portfolio assessment to the exclusion of teacher evaluation—which in a writing course is usually based on multiple drafts of many assignments. But under the right conditions, an exit assessment can support and enhance the teaching of freshman composition.

PROFICIENCY BARRIER ASSESSMENTS

Writing proficiency is one of those slippery terms that hide an even more slippery concept. Consider the variety of performance measures now in use. Some overachieving tots pass proficiency tests on alphabet blocks to win certificates at kindergarten graduation ceremonies; second-graders in my hometown must be able to identify punctuation marks and write their names to make it into third grade; high school graduates must be able to fill in a job application and write a paragraph with three complete sentences before the school board gives them a diploma; college students seeking to demonstrate that they need not take the required upper-division writing course at my campus of the California State University must write a three-hour documented comparison/contrast essay based on readings assigned in advance; prospective teachers in California and Oregon must complete two impromptu essays to set topics in an hour before they may begin their teaching careers. Although it is hard to imagine a single description that would apply to these various tests, they are all comfortably known as "proficiencies," and everyone seems to accept them in both theory and practice as authenticating writing ability. And their role as barrier tests, which must be passed if a student is to proceed, is generally accepted and endorsed as appropriate.

In many instances, the term *proficiency* seems merely to replace the workaday term *skill*—on the well-established bureaucratic principle that long words for simple concepts are more dignified than short words. But an additional sense of adequacy, sufficiency for a particular purpose, is conveyed by the word *proficiency*: A person who is *proficient* is demonstrably capable. The fact that some people who pass their "proficiencies" are *not* particularly capable—in fact, are at best minimally functional at a few skills—sometimes makes the terminology of proficiency testing seem pretentious. On some college campuses, the proficiency test that certifies student writing as sufficient for the bachelor's degree is actually less demanding than the freshman placement test; the proficiency test is in fact a minimal competency test of mechanics designed only to weed out the students most likely to embarrass the institution whenever they set pen to paper.

Because colleges and schools vary widely in their curricula, students, and faculty, it is not possible to suggest here the kinds of proficiencies appropriate at various levels. Indeed, the sensible law requiring proficiency testing for high school graduation in California specifically demands that each school district develop, define, and administer its own proficiency tests. In all instances, however, if proficiency tests are to be useful to the students, instructors, and institutions who must cope with them, they must be carefully developed along the lines I have been suggesting.

GOALS OF PROFICIENCY ASSESSMENT AT THE UNIVERSITY LEVEL

The extension of writing proficiency testing to the university level represents a relatively new phenomenon on the American educational scene. Comprehensive subject-matter examinations are, of course, traditional at the graduate and undergraduate levels, and placement testing has been common since Harvard began examining entering students in 1874. But only in the past twenty-five years has a special writing proficiency certification begun to be added to course requirements for the college degree—no doubt as a reflection of general discomfort with university educational standards. Sometimes these certifications take place as an added exit examination for freshman composition, as just described; sometimes they occur at the point of entry to upper-division standing ("rising-junior exams"); and sometimes they are graduation or degree requirements, to be completed after achievement of upper-division standing or even classified graduate status.

To people outside the university community, it might seem odd that the bachelor's degree should need the support of additional certification in writing skill; if a college degree does not in itself certify a high level of literacy, one might well wonder if it means anything at all. Nonetheless, in recent years, such upstanding members of the university community as the City University of New York, the Georgia State University system, and the California State University have felt it necessary to protect the quality of their degrees by a writing certification requirement. A moment's speculation about the meaning of this requirement will illustrate just how pervasive these matters have become. Two particular aspects of university admissions procedures have a great deal to do with this new requirement: the expansion of college opportunities to previously excluded groups and the expansion of community college programs that satisfy university requirements for the first two years of study leading to the bachelor's degree.

The advent of open admissions to the City University of New York in 1970 was only the most prominent example of the expansion of college opportunity over the past three decades (see M. J. Lederman, S. R. Ryzewic, and M. Ribaudo, *Assessment and Improvement of the Academic Skills of Entering Freshmen Students: A National Survey*. New York: Instructional Resource Center, City University of New York, 1983). The social forces behind this development are too well known to be repeated here, although the degree or permanence of institutional change these forces have brought about is by no means clear. (As we move through the 1990s, an odd and informal alliance between conservative politicians—seeking to reduce expenditures on higher education by reducing enrollments—and liberal faculty—seeking to protect educational quality under financial pressure by maintaining small class size—has begun to restrict access to higher education once again.) A substantial number of students who had either not experienced or not accepted English as a socializing discipline began to appear in college classrooms in the 1970s, even at the most selective institutions. (Every academic movement has its comic moments. One small college in the Ivy League was dimly aware that its attempt at diversity brought in first-year students who might not be wholly content with the reading material in freshman English, Milton's *Paradise Lost*; as a concession to what it imagined to be poorly prepared minority students in a special composition section, this college changed the reading in the name of relevance—to Milton's shorter poem, *Samson Agonistes!*) Less isolated faculties were faced with increased numbers of students for whom the conventions of academic written prose were a mystery and for whom the traditional freshman English course seemed inappropriate.

Responses varied. Some institutions, well aware that inexperience with the conventions of prose did not necessarily reflect an inability to learn, made few changes in the curriculum; they simply expected their new students to make rapid adjustments, sometimes with minimal counseling support. Other institutions, well aware that the same inexperience presented a serious handicap to students who would have to write papers for a traditional faculty, instituted a wide range of remedial courses (with placement testing) and support services. Meanwhile, a general decline in student verbal ability, suggested most dramatically by a precipitous decline in Scholastic Aptitude Test scores, added to the new populations a considerable group of traditional students without skill at academic writing. For these reasons and many others, it became much more difficult to enforce high academic standards in freshman English courses.

At the same time, more and more students were beginning their university work at community colleges; after graduating from these colleges and receiving certifications that they had completed all general education requirements, including writing proficiency, these students transferred to four-year colleges. Although the two-year colleges tended to take seriously their responsibilities for writing instruction and general education certification, many of their composition classes were occupied by large numbers of students who were not likely to proceed to four-year institutions. It became difficult for these community colleges to maintain standards, and the four-year institutions receiving their transfer students with writing requirements fulfilled became increasingly uncomfortable with such certification.

While these forces and others were diminishing the actual standards and the credibility of freshman-level writing certification, the universities were experiencing an increasing fragmentation of their curricula. Fewer students were majoring in the humanities and other liberal arts disciplines, and increasing numbers were pursuing majors that they felt would lead more directly to jobs in business and technology. Except at a few highly selective institutions, the traditional faculty consensus that writing well was important in all fields became less and less dependable. Teachers who assigned term papers or essay exams found increasing numbers of advanced students for whom such work was new and surprising. And employers began to complain more loudly than ever that degree recipients could not write as needed on the job.

Thus the new writing proficiency requirements at the university level represent a widespread belief that a student may complete course requirements for a bachelor's degree and still be unable to write at an acceptable level. The new certification requirements also assume, with somewhat less justification, that college can and should define a level of writing proficiency appropriate for all graduates and that such an achievement can be certified.

TYPES OF PROFICIENCY ASSESSMENTS IN USE

Various institutions have been implementing policy on the writing proficiency requirement in recent years, and it is instructive to review the procedures that are in use. As always, the assessment problems have turned out to be much greater than they were imagined to be, and every method of implementation has shown both strengths and weaknesses.

Multicampus Testing

The principal advantage of a large-scale proficiency test is its overall efficiency. Substantial resources can be brought to test development, administration, scoring, and analysis; participating campuses can realize the benefits of the test without incurring much cost. Such long-standing programs as the New York State Regents Examinations for high school subjects have demonstrated the advantages of establishing statewide standards of proficiency in various fields. Yet large-scale proficiency testing in writing is fraught with special problems. The statewide examinations for college students in Georgia and Texas, for example, have aroused substantial faculty opposition from those who find them insensitive and inappropriate for their particular campus or students. Because any definition of writing proficiency must be developed through discussion and consensus, and because a campus's standards for writing are a major component of that campus's educational quality, proficiency testing in writing perhaps should not be conducted on too large a scale.

The twenty-campus California State University (CSU) established a systemwide *placement* test for entering first-year students in 1977 but did not do the same for the graduation proficiency requirement established in the same year. The economies of scale that were obviously beneficial for the placement test seemed much less sure for the proficiency requirement. Educators responsible for establishing such a test had to ponder several questions: Is a test the best device for certifying writing proficiency for college graduates? What kind of test would certify writing proficiency over a wide range of campuses, majors, and professional programs? Can a single writing proficiency standard be established for English majors at San Francisco State, accounting majors at Northridge, animal science majors at Pomona, and forestry majors at Humboldt? In light of these questions, CSU simply required that each campus certify the writing ability of its graduates and left the method of certification up to each campus.

Of all writing tests, the proficiency test is the most political, the hardest to agree on, and the most dependent on instruction. The large-scale test gains uniformity of standards and certain economies, but it loses the nearness to instruction that alone gives the concept of college writing proficiency a meaningful context. Many faculty will argue that the best method of demonstrating writing proficiency is through the completion of a demanding course requiring a substantial amount of writing and rewriting, with some sort of coordination and assessment beyond the classroom to confirm consistency of standards. If such an instructional program cannot be instituted, another strong option is a portfolio assessment with wide participation by faculty from a range of disciplines. A writing proficiency program ought to encourage such methods of certification, for a series of writing samples will provide more reliable measurement than any one test can, and careful response and instruction during the course or after the portfolio review will lead to improved writing overall. A test can be a weak link in assessment and is generally an unsatisfactory alternative to instruction. The further a test moves from instruction, the more problems it accumulates, and large-scale writing proficiency testing is no exception.

These pedagogical and psychometric principles developed into a compelling argument against a large-scale proficiency test in California. If writing proficiency (the thing itself rather than the test) is the program's goal, responsibility for certifying that proficiency should be placed within the college curriculum, not outside it. That is, an assessment cannot in itself improve student writing; it can only at best lead to a strengthened writing instruction program. (I am frequently astonished at the view that an assessment will, by itself, improve teaching and enhance the results of education—as if a good fever thermometer could replace physicians and pharmacists and bring about good health.) If a test is entirely separated from the curriculum, it might not even do that, for such separation seems to turn the test into a hurdle to be gotten over rather than an important part of learning. For these reasons, the California decision to resist statewide certification and remand the requirement to the individual campuses in the state university system was sound. As these campuses have wrestled with the problem, they have provided laboratory cases of the variety of ways to implement such a requirement on a single campus. I list here some of the proficiency assessments that have been tried, with their advantages and disadvantages, concluding with the method that seems to me to be the best.

Campus Testing Programs

An individual campus faced with implementing a writing certification require-ment is likely to turn first of all to a single test. Particularly when the campus is large and complex, a test offers many advantages: a single standard, sometimes imagined to be "objective"; an addition to the quality control of the campus without the effort of reviewing or changing the curriculum; and a simple funding apparatus, a test fee. The test provides the answers, so there is no need even to raise the questions; everything looks deceptively simple. But the test is the beginning of problems, not the end of them. The extremely high stakes of a barrier proficiency test—which will deny some students the opportunity for further education or even the degree—makes the test into a major enterprise in itself. Special attention must be given to continuous test development, to student advisement both before and after testing, and to test security and cheating. Fly-by-night outfits are likely to appear in town the weekend before the test with expensive materials and cram courses in test taking. Students who have failed the test several times become increasingly desperate and, with only the test between them and their degrees, may tend toward increasingly desperate measures. Meanwhile, pressures to lower the standards of the test or to provide exemptions for an increasing number of special cases become almost irresistible.

At the same time, students who do not pass the test after one or two attempts and who seriously want to improve their writing will make continued requests for the establishment of a course to teach them the skills they lack. The result of such requests has been a new and appalling course: the *upper-division* "remedial" English course. Such courses are never called "remedial," as no one is willing to admit that the institution enrolls juniors and seniors who lack writing proficiency; hence, they are given a wonderful variety of pseudonyms: intensive English, grammar review, proficiency test preparation, and the like. With the exception of a few heroic and responsible faculty, the instructors of these difficult and unpleasant courses are generally those with the least experience, status, and knowledge.

Some administrators and faculty members claim that a single proficiency test, despite its problems, is still the most effective way to raise literacy standards on their campuses. As large numbers of students with particular majors fail the test, the faculty in those fields must recognize their responsibility to teach writing in their courses, and only the test can convey that message. But it is extremely difficult to include substantive matters on such a proficiency test, and the standards for scoring tend to become very low; after all, the test is an absolute barrier to the degree for a wide variety of students, and it is politically unwise to fail too large a percentage of graduating seniors. In addition, some inept students, unwilling or unable to take additional writing courses, may wind up taking the test repeatedly, hoping that some miraculous event will allow them to pass. The test poses special problems, not easily dealt with, for students for whom school English is a second language or a second dialect, and such students often cannot pass a timed essay test without special consideration. Essays turn up written by students taking the test for the ninth or tenth time. Not only is there an air of desperation in the exams of such students, but their recurrent papers serve to lower disproportionately the overall quality of test performance.

These examinations violate an essential general principle of testing: No single test is sufficiently reliable to be depended on, by itself, for a major decision about students. A second proposition is almost as important: When assessment becomes separated from teaching, both teaching and assessment suffer. And when passing a test begins to seem unrelated to learning, we ask our students to become cynical about learning itself.

Course Certification

The foregoing arguments are so compelling to some faculty committees and administrators that they decide to omit proficiency examinations entirely and depend wholly on certification by the course instructors. Students who pass particular courses will be presumed to be proficient writers, and that is the end of it. But that procedure is no more an end to problems than a test is. Again, new difficulties present themselves. Where is responsibility for the certification course to reside? Some campuses will decide to remand certification of writing proficiency to the department of the student's major. History majors should write well enough to please historians, engineers to satisfy the engineering faculty, and so on. But that decision tends to work out very badly, as many of these instructors know little about the teaching and measurement of writing, and some of them may be less than adequate writers themselves. Thus results tend to be so uneven as to diminish the requirement; some departments become very demanding, requiring a disciplinary writing course with high standards, while others become cynical and designate a course that may have no more than a single essay examination, if that. On one campus, a course in musical composition (designated by a satirical music department) and a course in computer programming (proposed by a naive math department) were supposed to satisfy writing proficiency requirements.

In an attempt to make such course designations more consistent and fairer to students, some campuses will establish guidelines for writing proficiency courses and even faculty committees and administrators to enforce the guidelines. (Such procedures sometimes lead to writing-intensive course requirements, a variation I take up next.) Unfortunately, with no common assessment or strong coordinator to hold together such a program, the centrifugal forces usually become too strong to resist. In departments with little or no training or interest in the teaching or assessment of writing, the program will relax into a series of departmental courses that may or may not involve writing and are taught by new faculty members. Therefore, some campuses with experience in this area no longer expect the academic departments to certify writing proficiency. All students must pass an English department writing course or a course administered by the English department. Although such a procedure reduces the problems of administration and inconsistency, it tends to confirm the destructive myth that only the English faculty need be concerned about student writing. In addition, it puts an immense strain on English department staffing, which usually must accommodate freshman composition as well, and diminishes the emphasis on the study of literature, which most English departments wish to maintain. The proficiency course becomes a burden to be borne by unwilling literature instructors, the English department alone is responsible for denying degrees to students approved by everyone else, and the rest of the faculty (whose lack of concern for student writing has spurred the demand for proficiency certification) are free to continue business as usual.

Writing-Intensive Courses

A popular variation on the course certification requirement is the establishment of an institutional "writing-intensive course" requirement. Every graduate must complete a certain number (usually two or three) of "W" or "WI" or "M" (for "Writing in the Major") courses, so designated in course listings; sometimes one or more of those courses must be taken outside the area of the student's major.

The "W" program often begins with a strong vote of confidence from the faculty and the administration, for its advantages are many and obvious. Faculty from throughout the university will be teaching the certification course, so responsibility for student writing is disseminated as it should be; faculty teaching the "W" courses will become so attuned to the power of writing as part of learning that they will carry that pedagogical understanding over into all of their teaching, even spreading the word to their colleagues; the writing course helps induct students into the discourse community of the major, an often neglected but important task; students will understand that writing is often required in courses that are taught outside the English department; instead of creating a new testing program or a new curriculum, the institution simply has to adjust existing courses to fit the "W" requirements. A simple adjustment of general education requirements takes place, and a cadre of enthusiastic faculty from a variety of disciplines volunteer to offer the opening set of "W" courses.

But the "W" program is filled with traps for the unwary and usually leads to unforeseen fiasco. For example, in the mid-1980s, a large state university in the East launched itself into writing across the curriculum in a well-publicized attempt to improve the thinking and writing of its graduates. The university senate required "W" courses to be instituted in each department; three "W" courses were required for the degree. The administration promised four kinds of support: a consistent faculty development program, an improved and supported writing center, enrollment caps of twenty for the "W" courses, and a long-term effort to support formative as well as summative assessment of the program.

Five years later, as evaluator of the program, I found the shambles of what remained of the ambitious and laudable design. None of the four administrative promises had materialized. The faculty development program and the writing center had been sacrificed to a budget cut, a new administration had felt no obligation to the assessment program, and the enrollment caps had been made the responsibility of each department chair, whose budgets depended on high enrollments.

At a meeting of the teachers of the courses, I heard that so few "W" courses were offered that enrollment pressures caused by the requirement had led to an average class size over fifty, that the faculty were angry and frustrated at being asked to teach writing with no support under such conditions, and that very little writing was going on in the (ironic laughter) writing-intensive courses. From the department chairs I learned that the weakest instructors and the least attractive courses had been designated "W," as the requirement ensured survival for both.

In a devilish twist, faculty teaching non-"W" courses had sharply diminished their writing requirements because their "W" colleagues were now supposedly teaching and requiring writing, thereby relieving them of that time-consuming responsibility. Even the most dedicated "W" teachers were doing more harm than good, as they had received no training in ways of using writing to assist learning. One physicist took me aside to tell me that he was devoting many class sessions in his "W" course to spelling and punctuation (though he himself had only the dimmest understanding of them), despite the demands of the class material and the lack of time to read student writing. I tried hard to praise him for his goodwill, but when I asked him if he had found a way to teach revision to his students, he looked surprised and puzzled, so I changed the subject.

I was not surprised to find, at a meeting with students, that some of them did not know what the "W" requirement stood for ("Work in Class"?). No assessment of the "W" program had been conducted and none was contemplated—and it was just as well. Recently, over a thousand graduating seniors had the requirement waived because insufficient "W" courses were offered for them. Net result of the new writing program: less writing throughout the curriculum, cynical faculty, mocking students, and graduates even less prepared to do critical thinking and writing than before.

But I have also seen a "W" program still effective after five years—indeed, becoming more effective as it matures. The University of Missouri (UM) in Columbia began modestly, with a single required "W" course, and in 1993 expanded that requirement to a second "W" course. As opposed to the eastern university, UM saw to it that the necessary support structures for the "W" program were protected and developed. The writing center is well funded, with professional direction, excellent facilities and staff, and a budget for tutors. Although UM does not require small classes for the "W" designation, classes that surpass twenty are budgeted for trained teaching assistants to help with the writing instruction. A powerful campus committee oversees the program, reviewing course curricula and insisting that its list of course requirements be included in the actual curriculum of each "W" course; these requirements include a minimum number of words for students to write, a minimum number of revisions, and a paper that debates issues in the field of the course. Most important, the university has continued to sponsor well-reputed seminars in writing, attended not only by the faculty but by various administrators as well.

Despite the high morale, continued support, and favorable reputation of the University of Missouri's "W" program, it is not free of problems. As the program expands, it is unclear whether the faculty will continue to volunteer a sufficient number of "W" courses to meet enrollment demand. And the program has not yet encountered an entirely new administration that may have different priorities. Nonetheless, universities like UM that take writing seriously can make a writing-intensive program work successfully. But no one should minimize either the difficulties or the expense involved over the long term.

Test with Course Option

Some campuses have tried to combine the advantages of certification through a test with those of a certification course. For example, students who fail the campus test are not required to keep retaking it until they pass; they might be certified as proficient despite a failing score on the test if they receive a passing grade in, say, English Z, "Intensive English."

The advantages of this procedure are clear. Most students will presumably pass the test and receive certification. Only the weakest students will need an upper-division writing course, so the staffing burden and expense for such a course are no longer overwhelming. If the test is responsibly run and the course well staffed, the quality of the college degree is protected without the necessity for every department to review its curriculum and without the elaborate structure of the "W" requirement.

However, this procedure ends up combining the worst aspects of both test and course certification. Because the test is the primary means of certification, all the pressures on the test will urge a higher passing rate and lower standards; the test will generally be seen as a minimum proficiency test, to be failed only by dumbbells. Thus all the problems of the single-campus test procedure will remain, with the one important exception that adequate writers who do not test well will now have a more appropriate route to the degree.

Meanwhile, it is hard to exaggerate the negative effects on the course that must be taken by students who fail the test. The resentment felt by the teacher assigned to teach the upper-division remedial class is usually matched or overmatched by the resentment of the students forced to take it. No one expects it to be a substantive class; some simulacrum of minimum competency is bound to be the goal. The (usually young and inexperienced) teacher is solely responsible for upholding university literacy standards, under great pressure from students who have managed to get by until now despite poor writing ability.

Thus the test with course option tends to be a depressing method of certifying students' writing proficiency. Both the test and the course behind it tend to be public embarrassments, euphemistically titled and attended with reluctance by everyone involved. One major urban university now lists between sixty and seventy-five sections of an upper-division remedial writing course each term and hires a trained corps of graduate students to teach this pedagogical oddity each year. The people involved argue that the course is well taught and essential, particularly for the large numbers of able students for whom English is a second language. Nonetheless, the test is exceedingly elementary, and the course hardly rises above the high school level despite its upper-division designation. One wonders whether the proficiency program in fact protects university standards or rather protects faculty throughout the university who neglect their own responsibilities toward their students' writing.

Portfolio Assessment

Peter Elbow and Pat Belanoff gave great impetus to portfolio assessment in writing when they began to publicize the proficiency program begun at the State University of New York at Stony Brook. In two articles (see the book by Belanoff and Dickson cited earlier), they demonstrated how a portfolio assessment team could replace test scoring for proficiency assessment at a good-sized university. The students were required to prepare a portfolio from their work in the composition class, and the class instructor was involved, but not predominantly so. In evaluating these portfolios, the assessment team was able to maintain consistency and reasonably high standards, with sensitivity to the differences among students and among faculty. The advantages of portfolios, which I set out in Chapter 7, were made evident, and the enhanced validity of the entire operation seemed clear. The Stony Brook program demonstrated that relatively large-scale portfolio assessment can be practical and enormously advantageous to the teaching program; it also demonstrated how difficult such an assessment is to maintain. Many other institutions, including New Mexico State, the University of Cincinnati, and Alaska Southeast, have developed portfolios for proficiency assessments, adapting the Stony Brook model to their own programs.

We probably will not know until the end of the century whether portfolios will overcome the enormous problems of cost and reliability to survive as a serious large-scale barrier proficiency assessment device. We do know that an institution that is willing to support portfolio assessment and has devoted leadership can develop a powerful and meaningful barrier proficiency assessment that supports the teaching of writing.

I encourage institutions that have decided to institute a writing proficiency barrier requirement to attempt portfolio assessment if the faculty leadership is willing to give a major effort for some years to the project—and if the resources are available. But I do urge caution, for all the reasons I outline in Chapter 7. In addition, assessment by a designated evaluation team has the built-in danger of separating assessment from teaching; the time-consuming reading of portfolios exacerbates that problem by reducing the number of participants in the assessment to a team of specialists willing and able to do the job.

Certification through General Faculty Involvement

Because student writing proficiency (however it may be defined) is a result of consistent attention by the general faculty to student writing and because the call for certification outside the curriculum reflects dissatisfaction with faculty standards, any truly effective certification program must involve the faculty as a whole. I am not speaking here of altering existing departmental offerings to form "W" courses but rather of establishing a separate course—as part of a university's general education requirements—to be taught by faculty in the disciplines. Such a certification program must assume regular and well-supported faculty development activities as well as an effective student writing center.

Most of the other methods of certification avoid the painful and political process of involving the faculty in fundamental curriculum change. Yet a felt need for a barrier proficiency assessment—the assumption on which we are proceeding here—ought to be seen as a demand for such change. Testing programs extraneous to the curriculum have problems because they treat symptoms and actively avoid dealing with root issues. Although a writing certification program that does not involve many faculty is relatively easy to put in place, it is also easy to dismantle when attentions or budgets drift elsewhere. Because no real changes are involved, the program tends to be more cosmetic than actual, despite the energy expended by the people committed to it. Even the "W" course program is largely extrinsic in that it involves additions to ordinary courses, and these additions can easily be dropped. Furthermore, because the only campus check on a "W" course is a curriculum review, no one can feel sure that students passing the course have demonstrated much writing proficiency.

An effective way to certify student writing proficiency at the college level is to require of all students a passing grade in a significant general education writing course at the upper-division level, a course with clear, common, and public standards. If such a course becomes an accepted requirement, no one will consider it remedial, and all the pressures on the course will urge substance and quality.

What appears to be the major disadvantage of this procedure turns out to be a substantial advantage: The faculty must be willing to include the certification course as part of the required general education program, at the upper-division level. Woodrow Wilson once complained that it is easier to move a cemetery than a university faculty, yet without such movement a writing proficiency program is bound to be an empty gesture. If the faculty as a whole is willing to assume responsibility for student writing and to demonstrate that responsibility by adding and respecting an upper-division general education requirement, the pressure for proficiency certification outside the curriculum is bound to disappear in time. The greatest success that a writing proficiency program can achieve is to become unnecessary; if most faculty members decide to require writing in their classes and demand high-quality work, so large a proportion of students will pass any barrier assessment that it will wither away.

Once a writing proficiency course is part of the required curriculum, many of the problems we have been describing become manageable. Staffing demands need not fall only on the English department but can be spread throughout the institution, with all the advantages of widespread concern for student writing. Coordination of the program remains necessary and difficult, but each institution can draw on its tradition of coordination, common course requirements, and common exit examinations for multisection general education courses. Most important, neither teachers nor takers of the course will have any incentive to debase it; it will in fact seem more like a senior honors seminar than a remedial writing course, and students as well as faculty will bring inventiveness and interest to it. One byproduct of such a course may well be more important than the course itself: Course instructors—which over time should include most of the faculty—themselves learn the power of writing as a means of learning and begin to incorporate writing into the rest of their courses. Students end up with repeated opportunities to write and revise their work throughout the curriculum, the ideal toward which all of these programs seek to move.

Experience has shown that a common essay examination or portfolio assessment is absolutely necessary if the centrifugal forces that are always at work on advanced courses are to be resisted. If the staff teaching the proficiency course each term must meet to plan, discuss, select, and grade a common examination or the portfolios of all students taking their classes, there will be a built-in corrective to the tendency to specialize the disciplinary content of the sections or to diminish the importance of writing. The assessment should be under the purview of a faculty committee that monitors the required course as well, a high-prestige committee that will help maintain the quality of the program through regular oversight of staffing, training, curriculum, and assessment.

Some students will be able to test out of the required course by demonstrating a high level of proficiency on a difficult written examination or through an expert portfolio. Such an examination or portfolio can be unabashedly demanding, requiring, for example, analytical skill and a substantial ability to use sources; to organize, demonstrate, and connect ideas; and to revise one's work. Because the standard means of certification is the required course, the pressures to depreciate the assessment will not be difficult to resist. As long as the course is seen as the basic certification device, the challenge assessment can be appropriately demanding, designed for the relatively few special students who clearly do not need the course. Perhaps those who pass can form a special honors seminar or in some other way build on their demonstrated writing ability. Failing the assessment is no disgrace, for few students pass and most do not even attempt it. Most important, the challenge assessment now sinks in importance and prominence to its proper place, subordinate to instruction. Though the test or the portfolio will, of course, call for several kinds of writing and show careful concern for validity and reliability, it need not carry the entire burden for institutional standards.

This procedure for certification, involving the introduction of a new general education requirement at the upper division and requiring assent from most of the faculty and participation by many of them, requires more than most universities are willing to give. Establishment of the program is likely to take years of committee work, debate, and compromise, and its maintenance calls for substantial resources and attention. Most of the university administrators and faculty concerned about the writing ability of their graduates do not want to confront the issue if it entails so much trouble; they will prefer instead to complain (often about English teachers or the high schools) or to think that a test will make the problem go away. Some administrators and department chairs will neglect to ask how students can complete some courses of study without competency in writing. Others will point out and genuinely believe that writing is an outmoded or minor matter compared with the real business of the university (whatever they take that to be). Still others will allege that certification of writing proficiency should be in the hands of the freshman English staff or the admissions office. Some may even regard the concern about writing ability as a passing fad, even now being replaced by worries about computer literacy and science training. For all these reasons, and many more, the stopgap and halfway measures I have been describing seem on many campuses to be a more reasonable response to pressures for certification of writing ability than the thorough reform that the required general education advanced writing course represents.

It is idle to imagine that the need for institutional certification of students' writing proficiency will disappear in the near future. Indeed, the democratic promise of expanded opportunity for less privileged populations and the renewed vigor of the community colleges should continue to provide most colleges in the United States with unconventionally trained upper-division students; there also seem to be no signs that specializing majors in the college curriculum will ask their advanced students to return to the core of the liberal arts. Further, there are no signs that elementary and secondary education will be able to make significant changes in the writing instruction or standards now in use, nor do the teacher training programs in the colleges and universities suggest that the needed improvements are even contemplated. Thus the demands for the certification of students' writing proficiency outside the curriculum will probably continue and increase. The people responsible for such programs would do well to build on the experience summarized in this chapter. In this area, as in most others, the close linking of assessment to teaching produces the most constructive solution to educational problems, which are never as simple as they appear to be.

SELECTED REFERENCES

Belanoff, Pat, and Marcia Dickson. *Portfolios: Process and Product.* Portsmouth, NH: Boynton/Cook, 1991.

Faigley, Lester. "Ideologies of the Self in Writing Evaluation." *Fragments of Rationality: Postmodernity and the Subject of Composition.* Pittsburgh: U of Pittsburgh P, 1992. 111–31.

White, Edward M. "Change for the Worse." *AAHE Bulletin* Nov. 1990: 1–4.

———. *Developing Successful College Writing Programs.* San Francisco: Jossey-Bass, 1989.

———. *Teaching and Assessing Writing: Recent Advances in Understanding, Evaluating, and Improving Student Performance.* 2nd ed. San Francisco: Jossey-Bass, 1994.

Williamson, Michael, and Brian Huot, ed. *Validating Holistic Scoring for Writing Assessment: Theoretical and Empirical Foundations.* Cresskill, NJ: Hampton, 1993.

CHAPTER 6

RESPONDING TO AND GRADING STUDENT WRITING

<>

Though there is much debate these days about the most effective methods of responding to student writing, there is a clear consensus about the *least* effective ways to handle student papers. Far too much of what teachers do with student writing is picky, arbitrary, unclear, or generally unhelpful. Unfortunately, most of us model our teaching behavior on the instructors we have had in school and college, and most of us have much more experience with negative or worthless responding than we do with effective patterns. Because of this modeling experience, we need to make conscious decisions about how we will handle student papers if we are to use the most appropriate methods for our own classes; these conscious decisions will help us avoid merely repeating what some of our instructors did to us.

We shouldn't press the analogy too far, but teaching writing has a lot in common with parenting. It combines discipline and nurturing, encouragement and warning, even perhaps love and hostility. There is a curious intimacy to the whole business, as we read student response journals, hold one-on-one conferences, and write notes to one another.

This parallel to parenting becomes particularly apparent as we consider how we have absorbed patterns of behavior without conscious awareness.

Unless we make a serious effort, we simply adopt the parenting or responding styles of our early experience. And some of those styles may have been destructive or even abusive. We have to become conscious of and dissatisfied with these ways of responding before we will consider replacing them.

This chapter will focus on the wide range of options teachers have for responding effectively to student papers.

PURPOSES AND EFFECTS OF RESPONDING

The educational purpose of responding to and evaluating student writing ought to be the same as the purpose of the writing class: to improve student writing. (We must serve one other administrative purpose, to screen out students who do not write well enough, but I will return to that gatekeeper function later.) We seek to improve student writing in many ways, but in responding to writing we have one overriding goal: The student needs to see what works best and least well in the draft so that revision can take place. Hence, it does little good for the instructor to judge writing or to grade writing without the kind of response that allows the writer to appreciate the reasons for that judgment. If the student can simply dismiss the teacher's views as mere personal opinion, the writing will not improve. Writers (like all learners) improve when they can internalize evaluation—when they can themselves see what needs to be changed and how to make those changes. Conversely, if the draft is truly finished (and very few are), the writer needs to see just where its excellences lie so that they can be repeated.

An analogy to learning in sports is appropriate, if not perfect. The batter in a batting cage or the tennis player at the service line hits the ball and gains an immediate response; if the ball goes awry, the player will make immediate corrections, steadily practicing until the ball goes straight. The coach closely observes the performance and offers suggestions, sometimes modeling the most productive behavior, but the player is the only one who can make the changes needed. It is patently absurd for the batter to blame the coach for his strikeouts or for the tennis player to ignore her game and strive only to please the coach. And no coach, however kind and supportive, can pretend that bad play will win; nor can an irascible and competitive coach gain improvement by continuous harassment if the player will not practice. Writing is, of course, more complex than most sports, and I will not pursue this analogy any further, but writing teachers can learn a good bit about teaching from watching a good coach.

Clearly, a grade on a paper, with no comment or only a cryptic phrase or two, will not add much to student learning. Sarcastic or harsh comments will allow the student to displace dissatisfaction with the paper (the teacher's intention) with dislike of the teacher and thereby short-circuit learning. Steady red-marking of all possible errors will bewilder and frustrate students, who cannot profit from an overload of correction; such papers tend to receive a cursory glance from the student before being thrown away. Puzzling abbreviations (*k, d, fs*) are abstruse to the student; they may mean "awkward," "diction," and "fused sentence" to the teacher, but for whom are they intended? Even generalized positive comments made by well-meaning softies ("Nice work," "I enjoyed reading this") frustrate students, who want to know what the teacher found "nice" and what made reading enjoyable. With so many teachers responding to student writing in such negative or uninformative ways, those of us who respond more professionally to student work can anticipate warm student appreciation and a genuine attempt to improve as we surprise them by taking their writing seriously and respecting it and them.

For many of us, in our student days, the writing and submitting of papers was part of the general antagonism inherent in education, the war between student and teacher. We did our best to figure out what the teacher really wanted, often puzzling for hours over obscure directions, or no directions, and using much creativity in what we called "psyching out" the professor. Then we would hand in the paper and hold our collective breath while we waited for more or less mysterious judgments to appear when the papers were returned. If we made mechanical errors, we could expect snarls, but we often received those snarls anyway for unpredictable reasons. However, we didn't complain much because in our heart of hearts we knew we were guilty of unknown sins. We didn't pretend to know "grammar," which was an impenetrable puzzle of arbitrary rules of linguistic conduct, and we thought that the teacher did and would punish us for our unintentional and inevitable violations. It was all part of the war, and, like Marine recruits, we expected random humiliation. The grade was all that really counted—revision was rarely required or rewarded—so we developed various ways of ignoring the comments a few teachers sometimes provided.

Since so many of these patterns remain, it is interesting to consider what purposes they served and continue to serve. At the onset, it seems clear that the pattern I just described *is* a pattern: Unclear assignment, harsh commentary, lack of expected revision, emphasis on grades—all add up to an exclusionary design, with concern only for product. In other words, this pattern rewards the academically canny and privileged, who can be depended on to know already what is being taught. The purpose of the grade and comment was to reward virtue and punish vice, and the moral overtones of the conflict led naturally to harshness. Students who did not show evidence of good writing were socially and morally offensive, wasting the time of the university and the professor. The teacher's red pen symbolized the scarlet letter, which on English papers was rarely an "A." It demonstrated the moral offense of the "errors" it excoriated and the pain of the teacher who was forced to mark them. Some instructors maintain this metaphor still in their conversation, unaware; they will talk of taking a batch of papers home for the weekend and "bleeding all over them."

What this pattern most obviously lacked was a concern for writing as learning, for the teaching of writing as supportive of learning. What it unconsciously enforced was the gatekeeper function of schooling, rewarding the privileged, and excluding almost all whose parents were of the wrong class, income, or national origin. Instructors who unrepentantly continue this pattern today claim that they are upholding "standards," as if it were somehow wrong to help students learn.

The concern for standards is real and important but should not serve as an excuse to indulge in negative responding patterns. An essential part of the writing teacher's job is to teach and enforce standards of performance that will allow students to succeed in college. This is the gatekeeper function of writing courses, an institutional (rather than educational) function that makes many instructors uncomfortable. Some large state universities make freshman composition virtually a wing of the admissions office, expecting the staff to winnow out the unqualified rather than to use university resources teaching them. The moral dilemma posed by such a situation is difficult indeed, and every instructor will resolve the conflict between teaching and selecting in an individual way; but this conflict should not lead to the use of evaluation and responding only as an administrative selecting tool. Nor should it lead to a narrow definition of writing as a mere test of certain skills that the institution may define as necessary.

The uses of writing are so large—as a tool for learning new material, as a means of power in a verbal world, as a way to understand complex ideas, as a route to understanding the self, and so on—that we do not want to narrow our purpose as writing instructors to merely judging and enforcing group standards. We must accept some responsibility for standards, for the sake of both the institution and the students who will be required to fulfill its demands. But if we accept the profound value of writing and its many uses, responding to writing becomes extraordinarily complex, calling for some special thoughtfulness on the instructor's part.

The pressures of time and the force of tradition often keep us from thinking through the purposes and effects of responding to a particular set of student papers. Most teachers proceed to "mark" a set of papers without much consideration of options. They read each paper through, red pen in hand, marking mechanical errors as they go, writing comments of one sort or another in the margins, and concluding with a grade and a comment justifying the grade at the end. Such a procedure can give sensitive and supportive help to students, for it demonstrates a careful reader's responses, but it does not make sense to respond to every assignment in the same way.

Must every assignment be graded—or be graded on the same scale? Must the teacher read and mark every word of every piece of writing done in a writing class? What is the point of marking careless mechanical errors on drafts that will be revised or that are not designed for a demanding audience? Are we taking ownership of the paper away from the student by our markings and asking the student to say what we want instead of what he or she wants? Are we sufficiently aware of what recent literary theory has taught us about the problematics of reading texts, including student texts? What are some useful ways of involving students themselves in the evaluation and response that every writer needs? How can we structure our comments, and student peer comments, so that students will want to revise their texts for their own sake rather than for ours? Questions such as these ought to arise before the red ink begins to flow. The answers to such questions should make the immense amount of time spent with student papers more productive, more interesting, and, perhaps, less time-consuming.

RESPONDING TO DRAFTS

Responding to writing does not begin when you start to read student essays; it starts much earlier, at the point when the assignment is made. Earlier chapters in this book have spoken at some length about the problem of devising appropriate writing assignments; we need only note here that a careful assignment makes the task of responding to the papers it elicits easier for the instructor and more useful for the student.

Perhaps the most useful responses of all occur very early in the writing process. The teacher may discuss the assignment and ask students to go through some prewriting exercises; some examples of previous classwork may be distributed and analyzed. Surely this is valuable. But more valuable still is the presentation by the student (to the class or to a small peer group) of early ideas for writing. The advantages of making such presentations are obvious: The student must gain ownership of the ideas presented, must get to work early on the task, and must come up with ways of demonstrating the major concept of the essay and making it interesting to others. The response to these presentations must be a delicate combination of support, encouragement, and rigor. If the topic is unworkable in toto or in the form presented, this is the moment to help the student see the problem, when there is sufficient time for a change. If the evidence is unconvincing or weak, the student needs to hear that from the teacher or from the peer group. But responses at this early stage need not be harsh, for their only function is to help the student do good work. No grades or editing issues (the nightmares of so many students) need enter here. Good responding practice will begin with class discussion of the assignment, continue with class or group discussion of individual plans for the assignment, and then move into a consideration of steps for revision.

We may talk about writing as discovery and revision and even schedule due dates for work in progress, but unless we build respect for revision into our evaluation of writing, our students will not believe us. If we continue to give a single grade for the finished (or unfinished) writing product, we are in fact saying that the product is all that we value. Therefore, the logic for rewarding the work in progress is compelling, and not only for the reasons I have been stating. Term papers, and student essays in general, are among the least valuable products in a world of waste paper; only a tiny percentage of them are saved, and only a minuscule percentage are published. True, they serve as products to be graded, but the only real reason for their production is as testimony to student learning. In many cases, that learning is better measured through the steps of production than through the final formal product alone.

This is a delicate balance, for too much grading simplifies responding and irritates everyone. Some instructors handle it by giving grades on one kind of scale for drafts, bibliographies, and the like—say, a numerical scale similar to that used in many holistic scoring sessions (typically, 6, high, to 1, low). The final draft can then be graded on the usual "A" to "F" scale. Others, concerned about the imposition of authority and ownership implied by constant grading, use peer group responses and a simple check-off system to note the completion of parts of the task. It all depends on the goals of the course and the assignment. But the central point remains: Any composition instruction that attempts to inculcate good writing habits should both require and respond to stages of the discovery and revision process.

We need to be careful about our real messages in this regard; if we intend to value revision as part of the writing process for everyone, we cannot treat revision as punishment for bad work. Unfortunately, numbers of well-meaning writing instructors include revision in their course plans either as an unpleasant option or as required only for bad work. Sometimes papers graded below "B" may or must be revised; sometimes revision is a possibility only if the students wish to raise their grades. In a great many classes, revision means merely editing for mechanics or making only the teacher's proposed changes. But every real writer and writing teacher know that revision means a "new vision" of what is being said, responding to internal as well as external demands; most writing in a writing class should be revised as a matter of normal routine, a natural part of the thinking process that writing expresses.

Whatever the grading or responding system, the comments on drafts should focus primarily on the conception and organization of the paper. There is no point in spending time on editing issues, aside, perhaps, from a note reminding the student that the final copy needs to be edited. Premature editing is the enemy of revision; some writers pay so much attention to spelling and punctuation that they neglect to attend to what they are saying.

To demonstrate that the ideas of the paper are what matter in early drafts, some teachers will require an outline of some sort to be submitted along with the draft, to make it easier for both student and teacher to see the ways in which ideas are developed. The basic job of draft writing is to discover and develop the subject, not to worry about mechanics. Hence, it is always helpful for the teacher to mark and respond to the clearest and most inventive of statements of the subject; this is another place for encouragement and stimulation of the student. If you are really bothered by errors in the draft, you might want to write something like "Be sure to clean up the copy after you revise so that readers will be able to understand and respect what you have to say." But red-marking the errors would be destructive at this point.

Experienced teachers have developed various schemes for reading early drafts and concentrating on their ideas, development, and structure. Some make a point of skimming the work before commenting, attending particularly to the opening and closing paragraphs; sometimes the first sentence of each paragraph will give a clear clue to the structure, or lack of structure, of the paper. It is always useful to identify the central or controlling idea, circle it, and comment on its interest and possibilities. Questions are more useful to students than assertions at this stage. Instead of writing "coherence" or "coh" in the margin, we might say, "I've underlined the two separate ideas you are pursuing in this paragraph; can you connect them? If not, focus on one or the other," or, "Your point in this paragraph makes good sense, but it seems to conflict with what you said in your opening. How do the two ideas relate?"

Finally, if we want students to profit from our reading, we should apply two commonsense rules: Do not overburden students with more commentary than they can handle, and find positive and encouraging ways to suggest improvements.

AUTHORITY, RESPONSIBILITY, AND CONTROL

One major difference between the teaching of writing and the teaching of other subject matter has to do with the role of the teacher. In most college courses, the teacher demonstrates authority (through expertness in the field), is responsible for the substance of what students are to learn, and maintains control over the course. However, each of these concepts operates differently in the writing course.

The teacher continues to exercise the authority that derives from knowledge and experience. The teacher knows more about writing than the students and has, of course, done more of it. The teacher is certainly a more practiced and skillful reader and is able to apply that skill to the reading of student texts. Therefore, the teacher has the authority to structure the syllabus, make assignments, and evaluate student writing. But students will not learn much about writing if they are merely passive recipients of the teacher's knowledge. Many studies support the need for active participation by students in the writing class if effective learning is to take place. Because the students must think their own thoughts, invent, discover, write, and revise, they must themselves develop some kind of authority; no one can write very well without having something to say, which implies a certain kind of authority over the material.

Thus the teacher must be willing to share some of the authority that comes inevitably with the instructor's role. If students are to write with a real voice, they must believe that they have, or can gain, authority over their subjects. When they write about personal experiences, that authority usually comes naturally enough: They are the only ones who really know what happened, and they have the right to speculate on what it means. But that tenuous sense of authority tends to disappear in the face of analytical assignments or printed sources. Frequently, students will merely describe what the assignment asks them to evaluate or summarize or quote someone's argument, even though the assignment asks them to relate it to their own or someone else's ideas. Adolescent assertiveness about everything turns, in college, to a trained unwillingness to take a stand or to claim authority before the "expert" professor or the printed source. Therefore, the writing instructor must find ways to help students understand the kind of authority all writers can claim (or earn). Some students simply cannot write for professors who assert, or seem to claim, too much authority over too many aspects of the material. I remember well a diligent student's hesitant question after I gave the class an assignment to write about a Renaissance poet: "Are we supposed to like Skelton?" Like many passive students, she had given all authorial authority (note the relation of the two words) to the teacher, or, more likely, I had unwittingly laid claim to so much authority that she saw no space to assert any of her own. Until I was able to convince her that her response to the poem was important and could not come from outside, she was voiceless.

Many conscientious writing instructors not only deprive their students of the authority all writers need but also unintentionally assume responsibility for the papers their students produce. The most obvious sign of this shifting of responsibility from the student to the teacher occurs when the student tries to revise an early draft in light of the teacher's comments. Almost invariably, the student will not change anything that the teacher left alone; all revisions focus on the corrections suggested by the teacher. The result is often very odd, sometimes considerably worse than the original. The revised portions of the paper are often much better, particularly if the instructor's comments led the student to rethink and reorganize his or her best ideas (as comments should). But the paper as a whole is now out of balance, with the original untouched portions, which seemed all right in the draft, now in need of work. When we say this, the student is often outraged: "You saw nothing wrong with it before!" In the student's eyes, and perhaps in our own, we have become responsible for some, or all, of the paper. "Is this what you wanted?" we may hear, as if it were now *our* paper.

The attitude we take in our comments is crucial here. We must convey to student writers that responsibility and control remain with them and that they need to do more than merely respond to our comments. We ought not to assume the role of editor for the student (marking every error is a common mistake, leading to student frustration or apathy in the face of too much red ink), nor ought we to tell the student what the paper should do. We should rather express any problems we perceive in the paper, point out the questions that the paper raises in our minds, and ask the writer to attempt to resolve these problems. We should always be friendly, even when we are feeling overburdened and crabby, and we should always find something to praise and encourage. At most, we might suggest some options or alternatives, but we must refrain from taking over the paper—even if we are convinced that we know just what it ought to be doing. As I suggested earlier, pointed questions are often more effective than assertions: "This seems to be your central idea; why does it first appear here, in the next-to-last paragraph?" "The second half of this paper seems to be on a different topic than the first half; which topic do you want to focus on?" "This original idea opens up exciting possibilities; can you find a way to examine them?"

A sensible posture to take toward drafts is to comment only on a few central matters: the ideas, the structure, the author's perspective or voice, for example. Certainly, sound pedagogy suggests that all comments contain something positive. Perhaps a comment about mechanics at the end ("The paper has sentence errors that ought not to appear in the final draft") might be useful in some cases. But good teaching is clear about goals; therefore, if we assume that substantial rewriting of the current draft will take place, we ought not to fuss about the spelling of words that may later be edited. We need to encourage risk taking in drafts, the trying on of ideas and arguments that may not work out or may turn out to be very exciting.

Finally, we have to have a healthy portion of humility in the face of student texts, even texts we have trouble respecting. After a decade of poststructural theory, we can no longer imagine that the text is a simple object or that our reading of it is somehow objective or neutral. We must be aware that the value of a text is negotiated, culture-bound, grounded in social structures. We come to student texts as we come to any texts, out of our own positions as people of a particular class, color, gender, age, and background. We respond as sensitively as we can, and we must finally record our evaluations on grade sheets, but the arrogance and arbitrariness of some teachers of the past might well be left behind along with their lessons in elocution and penmanship.

SAMPLE STUDENT PAPER IN TWO DRAFTS

I will reprint two drafts of a student paper written in response to the Analyzing Experience assignment given in Chapter 1. Here is the assignment the students received:

*Describe and analyze an institution or a group of some sort that you knew
well as a child: A school, school group, scout troop, dancing class, summer
camp, club, Sunday school—any group with an internally consistent set of
values you can see clearly—will serve. You have two specific jobs to accomplish: to describe clearly what it was like to be a member of the group at
the time and to assess from your mature perspective the meaning of the
group's values.*

Here is the first draft brought to class by Robert, a first-year student, whose
writing developed from discovery drafts about his Boy Scout Explorer post.
Robert felt that the paper was "finished" but not really satisfactory, and he read
it to his writing group with mixed feelings. I just happened to be sitting in
with the group.

Explorer Post 14: Not Intellectually Prepared

I was a member of Explorer Post 14 for two years. We were
a rather unorthodox Explorer post in that we wore no
uniforms, had a constitution, elected officers, and had a
nuclear physicist for a scoutmaster. Also, we did not go on
camping trips, hikes, and other things of this type that one
would normally associate with scouting. On the contrary, we
studied, heard lectures and saw films on math and science,
and worked on science projects, or at least that's what we
were supposed to do.

We actually did hear lectures and see films, but having
a serious discussion about any subject or working on a
project, that was out of the question. I believe that this
will become clear as I describe one of our typical meetings.

We would meet at Aerospace about 7:30 p.m. every other
Wednesday night. Before the meeting began there was always a
period of utter havoc. Loud talk and laughter, writing on the
blackboard, making paper airplanes and other juvenile

actions were common until the scoutmaster arrived. We then began the meeting with the flag salute, which was led by the president of the post. We quickly passed over the subjects of new and old business, project discussions, future plans, and other things of relative unimportance. We would then have a film or a lecture followed by a short, abortive discussion. This was not always the case. At times we did have lengthy intelligent discussions, but these were rare. Then we would adjourn the meeting and all go home. This is hardly the sort of meeting that would be expected of this type of group.

Another good example is projects. Each member of the group was expected to work on a project, individually or with another member. The only thing was, nobody ever worked on projects. With a group of this type, one would expect the members to be eager to work on projects and present them to other members for discussion, but this was just too much work.

I don't believe that the failure of our group to function as it was originally planned can be blamed on our scoutmaster as might at first be believed. On the contrary, I believe it was a direct result of the attitudes of the majority of the members toward doing anything that appeared to be work. Part of the members were the playboy type. They received good grades in school but preferred to chase around and go on dates three or four times a week rather than spend a little extra time working on a project or preparing a topic for a general discussion. Others were just plain lazy. All of the members had above average intelligence and the ability to

think and reason, but thinking was just too much like work.
Thus it appears to me that the members of this group were not
intellectually prepared for an Explorer program of this type
as it was originally designed.

Responding to "Explorer Post 14:
Not Intellectually Prepared"

The writing group began by praising the paper, which fulfills the assignment
quite well. Though it is weak on description, it does give a sense of what it
was like to be a member of the group at the time, and the writer does analyze
and point out the significance of the description. Since the first task for the
group was to point out what was done well, they praised Robert for using
enough detail to give them a sense of the scout troop. But along with the
writer, the group was not really satisfied with the paper, though they struggled
to figure out why.

I suggested that they look closely at its tone, the relationship of the writer
to both the reader and the topic. Freshman writing groups tend to be particularly
sensitive to tone, for many young students are at an age when nuances of
feelings have become particularly important. They noticed a conflict between
the Robert they knew and liked as a person and the harsh, judgmental tone
of the essay he had written. They pointed out some of the terms and phrases
that establish his relationship to the troop: "that's what we were supposed to
do" (paragraph 1), "that was out of the question" (paragraph 2). They also
pointed out some problems with the writer's attitude toward the reader, asking
the reader to condemn the other boys in the troop without much real evidence.
An acute listener in the group had noted that the fourth paragraph begins
"Another good example is projects" ("good example of what?"), which sounds
like a whine, as if there were a list of petty grievances. "You seem so stuffy
and hostile to the other guys," another student in the group said. "Didn't you
like them at all?" Robert protested that he liked the other boys at the time and
was still friends with many of them. Others in the group pointed out that
Robert was a warm and accepting person, not at all like the tone he took in
the essay, and wondered why he took the attitude he did; after all, the group
was a Boy Scout troop, not a seminar of rocket scientists. Robert thought for
a while and then smiled.

"I was trying to find something important to say, a controlling idea like Professor White here says we need. I guess I really forced things." He agreed with the group that the tone rang false; he had taken an attitude toward the boys in the troop that he really didn't feel, and that led to a false attitude toward the reader as well. He didn't much like the voice in the paper either.

Yet he felt sure that he had a good topic in the paper, even though he hadn't yet found a good controlling idea. The group went on to talk about scout troops and how they help kids find out who they really are. Robert joined in, saying that every scout troop is a kind of "explorer" troop in that they help their members explore themselves as well as their world. "Now *that's* an interesting idea," one of his friends said. "Why don't you go with that?" I concurred that the idea of exploration sounded promising as a concept for the next draft.

"I think I'll try it," Robert replied. A week later he had completely revised the essay, as follows.

Explorer Post 14: The New World

Explorer Post 14 customarily met in a room at Aerospace usually used by scientists to discuss such vital subjects as defense projects and space exploration. The walls of the spacious, well-lighted room were blank, except for the west wall, which was decorated by a map of the world showing all of the routes taken by the early explorers to the New World. But this map was covered by a large motion picture screen whose pale blankness gave the room an air of sterility.

The twelve sixteen-year-old boys supposedly gathered together for the purpose of exploring the world of math and science. But actually this was just a guise for their real purpose——the exploration of the novel, quick-paced world of the teenager.

The meeting began, supposedly, with the flag salute. Actually the meeting began fifteen minutes earlier as the group gathered in the room that was to be their uncharted

world for the next hour and a half. In these first fifteen
minutes, the initial exploration began with the boys testing
each other with silly comments about the day's activities at
school and home. W. T. Jones III, the leader of the particular
expedition, pulled the blackboard out to the middle of the
room and began to map out their course. As it turned out, the
map resembled the figure of Julia Roberts and therefore was
appropriately named The Temptation. About this time, Dr.
Nevin, the nuclear physicist/scoutmaster, entered the room,
and the expedition reached a temporary impasse.

After the flag salute, the lights went out and the motion
picture screen flashed with brilliant colors and the blank
walls reverberated with the sounds of a film titled *The
Exploration of the Planets and Beyond*. It was the story of the
astronauts and spacecraft that were venturing into the black
reaches of space to explore the Earth's nearest neighbors,
Mars and Venus. As the film ended, the bright lights again
flicked on, and Dr. Nevin engaged the boys in a discussion of
space exploration that lasted about twenty minutes.

But then the inevitable happened. The screen came down,
revealing the world map. The temporary impasse overcome, the
boys returned to their exploration with more vigor than
before. Their path led them to cars, the date W.T. had had the
night before, and girls in general. But soon they were forced
to end their journey, for the meeting was at an end.

During the last part of the meeting, Dr. Nevin had just
sat with the boys, laughing with them and only occasionally
entering a comment of his own. Why had he done this? Why

didn't he try to make the boys continue their discussion along more intellectually oriented lines? The reason is simple. He understood that in the strange, exciting world of the sixteen-year-old, self-exploration is much more intriguing than a journey into the world of science. For it is at this age when a person must find himself so that someday he will be a mature individual both mentally and physically. So each week Dr. Nevin took up the role of a silent guide so that a group of sixteen-year-old boys could engage in the exploration of life.

Responding to "Explorer Post 14: The New World"

The major changes from the first version to the second occur in the writer's attitude toward the boys in the scout troop and, consequently, in the controlling idea for the essay. The almost ritualistic condemnation of the boys, sometimes inappropriately bitter in the earlier draft, changes to one of sympathetic understanding as a result of more careful analysis and more original thought. As the writer examines his attitude toward the boys, he plays with the nicely ambiguous value of the "space exploration" of his topic: Adolescents are inevitably involved in exploring their own worlds, even when they are supposedly finding out about planetary space. Perhaps the scout leader knew what he was doing after all.

In my written response to this draft, I praised the revision for its new depth of thought. I made some notes in the margins, showing that I noticed the more understanding attitude the writer takes to the boys in the scout troop in the revised draft. I also noted the changes in the writer's relationship to the reader: "Instead of asking us to condemn, you ask us to understand," I wrote. I also noted in the margins that the details are now richer and focus on reactions on his controlling idea, whereas the previous draft had fewer details and only general connections between the descriptions and the controlling idea.

In my end note, and in a conference with Robert, I praised the changed organization, most obviously the new opening paragraph—which, Robert told me, had been the last part of the paper to be written. (I had mentioned in class that writers often write their openings last, after they see what their best ideas have turned out to be.) I did mention that the tone of the opening did not match the rest of the paper, but I tried to keep the emphasis on what it accomplished. Because Robert had decided to make connections between the exploration of outer and inner space, that controlling idea had to be kept alive throughout the paper—not an easy task. Further, in both drafts, the paper takes us through a troop meeting from beginning to end, so the organizational changes had to occur in the development of the idea, not in the chronological order of events. In both drafts, the closing paragraph presents the writer's analysis of the meaning of what has been described, but they are entirely different. In fact, I decided, with Robert's permission, to duplicate his essay to illustrate for the class the ways in which well-structured papers used opening and closing paragraphs to set tone as well as topic.

Here is what I wrote at the end of the paper:

> Robert, this is an excellent revision of your earlier draft—which was good work to begin with. You have focused your details on your new controlling idea, which is more convincing and satisfying to me than the condemnation that ruled the previous draft. You have also used the controlling idea to *control* the organization of the paper, to focus its elements.
>
> As you prepare this paper for your portfolio, you might want to see if you can harmonize the tone of the opening paragraph with the rest of the paper and if you can develop your idea of exploration more fully. Can you give us more details about the "self-exploration" you only suggest in this draft? I am impressed at the way you have improved your writing and look forward to what you might do with this interesting essay.

Because I require further revision of second drafts for certain assignments, I include some suggestions for improvement even on the best papers. Indeed, I find that most people are more interested in improving their best writing than their worst. Despite its insufficiencies, Robert's second draft remains well written and interesting, with a defined thesis about an interesting topic. Some writers might consider this draft only a first step on the path to a publishable essay, but most American college instructors would be very pleased to see work as good as this. My response in conference to the student, who was, after all, a first-year student, was "Bravo!" and a grade of 6 on the 6-point scale. Then we spent some time in conference talking about all that was well done in the paper and how he could duplicate the process for other papers. In fact, I asked for a reflective letter on his writing process for this paper to be included in his portfolio at the end of the term, as a way for him to have a record of his successful procedure.

COLLABORATIVE WRITING

In one sense, all writing is collaborative: Every writer needs some kind of audience, some conversation, some reading, some responding. The peer groups that are now part of many writing classes serve as sounding boards for initial ideas, responders to drafts, and even editors for presentation copies of final drafts. The picture of the writer as a solitary genius, holed up in an attic, emerging on occasions waving a manuscript that expresses his or her inner self, has not been a useful one for writing instruction. Far better is the wry comment that Hemingway is supposed to have made when asked about his times of greatest inspiration: "Nine to five on weekdays." Writing takes place all the time, among or even with other people. In fact, much of the writing done outside of the university (and, increasingly, in the university) is now actually accomplished by teams; collaboration in the writing of reports and papers has become more and more common. We see this concept in physical form in the newer configurations of computer writing laboratories, where groups of computers and collaboration software impose collaboration as a matter of course.

Collaboration offers special challenges and possibilities to the writing class. Some instructors regularly establish teams to produce papers: The teams allot portions of the tasks involved to their members, compile the drafts, and submit a single paper for evaluation as written by the team. Those who espouse this procedure claim that student involvement is much higher than in more traditional writing classes and that the results are much more satisfactory. Classes using the computer as a normal means of text production slip naturally into the collaborative mode, as an extension of networking and regular commenting on electronic texts. In some fields, such as business or science, collaborative writing is becoming so much the standard that writing courses that ignore team production seem old-fashioned. But establishing a curriculum and writing assignments for collaborative groups requires a complete rethinking of the writing course and may pose insuperable problems for commuter campuses.

Responding to collaborative writing offers challenges that have not yet been well resolved. Is the writing workshop approach, with teams going about their writing and responding to the work of other teams, too unstructured for college writing courses? Will students leaving such a class be well prepared for the individual production of term papers, theses, or other college work? Is it fair to give a high grade to each member of a team if only some of its members actually did the writing, be it ever so excellent? Is it fair to give a low grade to each member of a team if some excellent writers on the team have been insufficiently influential in determining the quality of the paper? Can the team members themselves give differential grades to their own members?

As with other innovations in writing instruction (such as portfolios), collaborative writing offers unusual opportunities to inventive teachers. In the course of the next decade, accumulated experience with this mode of teaching will help us find ways to meet the challenges of a shifting emphasis from individual to group writing, challenges only now emerging. The increasing use of computers for writing makes it likely that we will see more and more collaborative writing in all composition classes as time goes on.

USING STUDENT RESPONSE GROUPS

Whether or not we choose to allow or require collaborative writing in class, we might well consider using student response groups as a way of expanding the audience for student work beyond the teacher's desk. When the teacher is the only audience, students inevitably personalize the response; instead of working to improve their writing, they work to please the teacher, which is a much less valuable goal. And instead of internalizing writing standards, they will wait for the teacher's judgment before assessing their own drafts.

Although the basic reason for establishing student response groups is to provide this additional audience, other reasons also make the use of student response groups valuable in class. The social nature of a small group adds to the trust and comfort of the class; students enjoy working in small groups and getting to know one another. They also learn more from one another than we suspect. Students may be used to hearing, and ignoring, teacher complaints about mechanics, but they have to attend to some of their peers' saying, "This is really a mess; I just can't read it." As they explain their ideas and their evidence to a small group, they find themselves understanding and changing preliminary views; as they tell each other why they like or don't like drafts, they are forced to use the vocabulary of writing assessment in an active way. Even large lecture classes profit from some small group work, which enforces the importance of active rather than passive understanding.

As some students will find group work initially uncomfortable, we must establish the goals and procedures of student response groups in advance. And we cannot assume that students from all cultures will respond to group evaluation as positively as many students in American colleges do; students from some cultures find group work threatening, even bewildering, if their culture forbids verbal criticism out of a need to save face. Furthermore, students from any culture without experience in assessing their own work and who expect the teacher to provide all judgments may simply transfer that expectation to the group, thereby intensifying their writing apprehension. Simply asking groups to read and respond to each other's work may lead to useless ("I really like this") or destructive comments. Most students will follow the patterns they have learned in school, unless instructed otherwise, and will focus on mechanics or other real or perceived mistakes. They need to be instructed to focus on positive and useful responses (for example, "What is most successful?"), and you should provide models. Also keep in mind that students cannot do too many things at once ("Attend to these three questions"). These issues require that the teacher think through just what the groups can be expected to accomplish and how.

Different teachers with different teaching styles will use small groups in different ways. For example, for teachers using collaborative writing, small group work begins with the assignment itself, as the group parcels out different tasks for its members. The group is itself at the core of the writing process and must meet regularly to assess the progress and quality of its own work. When the assignment is completed, the group receives the grade.

Other teachers will use student response groups as part of a force for what literary theorists call reader-response criticism. This theory assumes that readers create as well as respond to a text. Thus it is essential for writers to hear what a variety of readers perceive as they make their way through the text. The writer must not be defensive or argue for his or her intentions; the writer's job is to be silent and take notes as members of the group detail their movement through the piece of writing and their reactions. If the writer would like to produce a different set of reactions, revision is called for.

Still others ask student groups to function descriptively: to describe to the author what they see as the controlling idea of the piece of writing, what its assumptions and arguments are, and how they understand it to be organized. Yet other teachers focus on evaluation, with the group emphasizing suggestions for revision. And still other teachers use the group simply as a means of socializing students into the college community of writers.

Here is an example of using groups for a limited purpose, to give a response to the writers of a personal experience essay. Though the example only suggests the wide range of possibilities for group work, it shows that student groups can be an important part of the response to writing that all authors need.

The first placement or diagnostic essay in this book (see Chapter 3, p. 50), calling for description of a character from childhood using detail that will convey an emotion, is ideal for group discussion. The groups, which should not exceed five students (four is ideal), can be instructed to read or listen to each person's paper and to write down the emotion that the writer evokes; each student should identify one part of each paper that evokes the emotion most clearly. After everyone has read or heard the papers, each writer calls for discussion of his or her paper, writing down the responses of each member of the group to the two tasks at hand without being defensive. The group should not spend much time hearing what the writer "really meant to say"; the writer needs to hear what the group has heard the paper say. The inevitable comparisons and dissonance in the group give the writer a clear sense of the relative success of the paper and of possible revisions.

Each assignment and each draft lead to different possibilities for group work. Sometimes, instead of a group of four, you will want to use pairs of students. You may want to reshuffle the groups so that patterns of response do not become fixed or too personalized, or you may want to maintain groups that are working well to cement their supportive function. And you may well want to develop a sensible mix of group work with full-class work, just as you will probably rely on groups more heavily for drafts than for presentation copies of student work. If you have a heavy student load, you may want to use group responses for early drafts that you will not read so that you can devote your reading time to more finished work. If your campus is computerized, you may use computer groups as well as class groups, and you may be able to insist that drafts be subject to spelling checkers or group editing before you read them.

Teachers unaccustomed to writing groups sometimes imagine that students will be unwilling to share their work with others or that they will value only the teacher's comments. Rare is the student who cannot work in a group because of personality difficulties, and though students from some cultures may present special problems, faculty who have begun to use groups find that most students are more willing to revise and to meet deadlines if they know that other students will read their work. Student responses may not be professional, but under professional guidance they can be helpful and less threatening than teacher responses. And students are less tolerant of inflated or pretentious language than many teachers are; a student comment of "Cut the bull" can serve as a healthy check on the usual student perception of "what English teachers like to read." Most important, the student response group offers a range of responses to the student paper, making it seem more significant and more worthy of attention. These responses dramatize our message about sensitivity to audience, offering a "real" audience in addition to the teacher, and also reinforce the ultimate responsibility of each writer to make appropriate revision decisions. Students almost invariably report that the most valuable activity in class is the group work they regularly undertake.

FOSTERING SELF-ASSESSMENT

Writing groups work powerfully to help students develop the ability to assess their own work, to understand that readers respond more positively to some portions of the text than to others, to see what works and what does not, and to help them read their own writing (not merely what they intended to write). But we must be aware that self-assessment is a painful and difficult process for students—as it is for teachers, whose resistance to evaluation is legendary. And yet without self-assessment, students will not revise or will do so reluctantly and without the requisite personal involvement. What else can teachers do to foster self-assessment?

One place to start is the writing log or journal, a place for thinking and discovering but not for finished work. The writing log becomes not only a mine for writing ideas but also a place for writing that is not fixed in form, including discovery drafts. One important difference between the working habits of skilled and unskilled writers is that unskilled writers hate to discard anything from an early draft, whereas skilled writers are always cutting and rearranging their work. The writing log, unlike a more finished draft of a paper, will not trap students into thinking that the writing is carved in stone; indeed, if the log is kept on disk, it is as evanescent as electrons. The more experience students have with less fixed forms, the easier it is for them to think of early drafts as material to be reworked, reviewed, reshaped, and revised. The basis of their revisions must be self-assessment, but the very idea of revision is supported by the existence of the writing log.

More direct support for self-assessment comes from work in class using scoring guides and sample student papers. A writing class will enjoy ranking a set of papers, such as those given in Chapters 3 and 4, according to a scoring guide. The exercise is more successful if the writers of the papers are from some other class, but it does work with class assignments as well. The central ingredient in such work is the scoring guide, which some teachers develop through class discussion to emphasize group ownership of the standards. Most students, in their heart of hearts, believe that teacher evaluation of writing is mysterious, subjective, unaccountable, and arbitrary. (Research in the subject agrees with the students.) Such a belief devalues revision, for there is no way to know if the revision will lead to a better grade even if the new draft seems better to the writer. But a public scoring guide, used consistently by the instructor and by the class as a whole, fosters self-assessment as well as group assessment and encourages revision. A student with an essay scored 4 can see why it is better than a 3 and why it is not as good as a 5; if asked to revise the essay so that it can be scored 5, most students will succeed in doing so.

Public scoring guides and class involvement in scoring clearly foster self-assessment and revision. Further, writing groups can serve as evaluators as well as support groups. Some instructors use class grading extensively, asking groups to grade the work of writers outside of their own group. This separates the support of one's own writing group (which provides coaching for revision but no grading) from the grading of papers from a different group (which provides assessment alone). But these valuable activities depend on clear public standards, which students not only understand but also agree with and enforce; when they apply those standards to their own writing—when they ask the same questions about their own writing that they do about the other papers they are grading—we get genuine revision.

Finally, there should be space in every writing course for writing that is not evaluated so that students can use writing to explore ideas, feelings, memories, and creativity without worrying about others' judgments. Whether that space is in writing logs, early drafts, proposals for papers, or even oral reports, such opportunities emphasize that the most important audience for all writing is the author, whose thinking is temporarily fixed on paper. When revision takes place to please *that* audience and seeks to meet internalized high standards, the writing course has done its job.

HANDLING THE PAPER LOAD

There is no point in denying it: Teaching writing courses or using plentiful writing in any course requires a substantial investment of time. Whatever devices we may use to reduce the paper load, we must from time to time sit down and go through piles of papers, responding as sensitively and intelligently as we can. But after granting the inevitability of such work, we are entitled to use all reasonable ways to reduce the paper load. The teacher who regularly works a ninety-hour week, spending every waking moment grading papers, is a grim cliché; such teachers in time either leave the profession in despair or lose the humane perspective a writing teacher should reflect. We, no less than our students, need to "get a life," and we must preserve some time for ourselves.

Briefly, here are a variety of methods for handling the paper load without overwork:

- Require student writing logs, which you can skim and respond to without editing or grading.

- Design writing assignments with care, present them in written form, and distribute samples of excellent responses so that students will hand in better work requiring less response time.

- Include assessment criteria along with assignments so that you can more easily point out to students where they are successful or not.

- Use student writing groups to give responses to early drafts or even to grade later drafts.

- Assign writing, such as journal entries, five-minute writes, or freewrites, that you will not need to read.

- Resist overmarking, proofreading, editing, and red-marking, particularly on drafts.

- Use scoring guides, the 6-point scale, and class discussion of sample papers to develop student self-assessment and reduce the need for extensive comments on individual papers.

- Focus written comments on papers to a few main points, raising questions rather than proposing solutions.

- Designate a limited number of papers for presentation level and grading.

Teachers of writing will continue, I am convinced, to work longer hours than most other faculty and to spend more time with their students as well as with student work. Most of us do the job because we genuinely enjoy such work and the intangible rewards such human contact brings. We have the means to keep our working hours within reasonable limits, however, and the suggestions in this book will, I hope, help on the practical end.

PRESENTATION COPY

Not every piece of student writing need be revised and edited to a high level of polish. Some students will have little trouble editing their final drafts to near perfection, but most students find this an onerous and frustrating task, particularly if they did not grow up in homes speaking the school dialect. If we have many students for whom the preparation of final drafts is a major task, we may want to specify the level of polish necessary for each assignment. After all, most of us are content with less than top performance in many aspects of our lives, even though we might be able to do a first-rate job when absolutely necessary. Some teachers feel that every essay should demonstrate the highest level of polish and that such a demand shows high standards, even though few students will meet the demand. But I think it is equally demanding, and more sound pedagogically, to identify certain essays as requiring high polish and then to insist on it; other essays, particularly drafts, can be submitted in less perfect form.

If we can be content with some work from each student that never enters final draft, which we could grade for stated criteria that do not stress high polish, we can be particularly demanding on the work that will reach presentation level. Our students need to know just what is involved in presentation-level work, including standard citation form and clean mechanics, and they need enough practice in producing work at this level so that they—and we—know that they can turn it out when needed. But they also need to know that writing is much more than editing and that clean copy is not equivalent to good writing.

When the essay is to reach the presentation level of polish, we can use all of our editing skill to work with students: Our responses will be detailed in every way. And we will ask students to keep producing drafts until the writing has achieved a high level of polish. I will do this on a few essays per semester but resist asking that every paper be brought to presentation level; we have so much to do, and writing offers our students so much beyond editing, that I am content to know that they can do high-level work, even if they do not do it all of the time.

CONCLUSION

The challenge of responding to student work is not only in rendering fair judgments (as we have learned through the paraphernalia of essay testing) but also in coaching and fostering the process. Most faculty have not thought much about the wide range of responding options they have, and so they repeat the patterns they experienced as students. But many of those patterns are useless or counterproductive, and other ways of responding can be extremely valuable to students, even though they may be less time-consuming for teachers. Thoughtful responding to student writing begins with a careful written assignment, discussed thoroughly in class, perhaps with examples and scoring guides. As the student essay moves through prewriting and drafts, the teacher must keep responsibility with the writer, even as student groups and the teacher respond to the sequence of drafts. Editing for high polish and grading of final products may occur, but responding to student writing includes the entire range of support that teachers, acting as coaches more than judges, can give students. The result of such teaching will be students more ready to revise, more willing to see writing as a form of critical thinking, more aware of internalized assessment criteria, and more ready to be responsible for their own learning.

SELECTED REFERENCES

Anson, Chris M. *Writing and Response*. Urbana, IL: National Council of Teachers of English, 1988.

Beginning Writing Groups. Produced by Wordshop Productions. 1991, videocassette.

Freedman, Sarah W. *Response to Student Writing*. Urbana, IL: National Council of Teachers of English, 1987.

Gere, Anne R. *Writing Groups: History, Theory, and Implications*. Carbondale: Southern Illinois UP, 1987.

Greenberg, Karen, Harvey Wiener, and Richard Donovan. *Writing Assessment: Issues and Strategies*. White Plains, NY: Longman, 1986.

Lawson, Bruce, Susan S. Ryan, and W. Ross Winterowd. *Encountering Student Texts: Interpretive Issues in Reading Student Writing*. Urbana, IL: National Council of Teachers of English, 1989.

Porter, Jeffrey. "The Reasonable Reader: Knowledge and Inquiry in Freshman English." *CE* 49 (1987): 332–44.

Student Writing Groups. Produced by Wordshop Productions. 1988, videocassette.

White, Edward M. "Poststructural Literary Criticism and Responding to Student Writing." *CCC* 34 (1984): 186–95.

CHAPTER 7

USING PORTFOLIOS: DEFINITIONS, STRENGTHS, AND WEAKNESSES

━━━━━━━━━━━━━ ⟨⟩ ━━━━━━━━━━━━━

A portfolio is a folder or binder containing examples of student work. For generations, some faculties in the fine arts have been using portfolios for assessment and grading; the final examination in a class in drawing, painting, or architectural design, for example, will often consist of a portfolio of the student's work, which will be displayed, critiqued, and graded. Some writing teachers have used portfolios in the same way in their writing classes, and in recent years some writing programs have done the same. Because the use of portfolios for assessment is very attractive, many schools and colleges have begun using portfolios for all kinds of purposes: screening students for advancement, assessing general education program outcomes, evaluating instructors, providing students with employment dossiers, and so forth. Though I cannot address all possible uses of portfolios, I will summarize their strengths and weaknesses and look at a number of their possible uses in writing programs.

The great advantage of portfolios for assessment is that they can include numerous examples of student writing, produced over time, under a variety of conditions. Unlike multiple-choice tests, they can show a student's actual writing performance; unlike essay tests, they can showcase several kinds of writing and rewriting, without time constraints and without test anxiety. Whereas most evaluation instruments provide a snapshot of student performance, the portfolio can give a motion picture. Some programs enhance the meaning of the portfolio by allowing (or requiring) revisions at the time of submission so that students can appear at their best and can demonstrate to themselves as well as to their readers what they have learned to do. And if one requirement of the portfolio is a self-assessment or reflective essay, students wind up taking responsibility for their own learning.

Early reports on assessment from experiments with portfolios are very positive. Unlike any test, students usually find the preparation and self-assessment of portfolios to be inherently meaningful and worthwhile as a record of work they have done and want to keep. They do not feel that way about tests. At the end of the term, only a few students will come around to pick up their final exams (if they are made available), but virtually all will make an appointment to retrieve a writing portfolio. Why? Exams are by their nature external, usually a mere testing device for the benefit of the instructor and the institution. But students *own* their portfolios, particularly if they have revised and tended them for months or years.

The problems with portfolios as measurement devices emerge from their sheer bulk, the uncontrolled conditions under which they are produced, and the difficulty of achieving consistent scores. The mass of portfolios can be daunting. Even twenty or twenty-five portfolios at the end of one writing class form a formidable pile of papers, over one hundred thousand words to read. Several classes or an entire freshman composition program multiply the quantity, of course, and some institutions require each student to compile a portfolio throughout the college years, the reading and evaluation of which is a truly massive undertaking. The uncontrolled conditions for portfolios pose another set of problems. Because it is difficult and inappropriate to supervise closely the production of the portfolio contents, several validity problems are inevitable: A weak student with no outside responsibilities will be able to produce a more substantial portfolio than a better writer who happens to be a single parent supporting a family (a timed test evens out the measurement conditions); and students are likely to get help of various sorts (from consultations in the writing center to purchased papers from unscrupulous commercial firms), so it may be hard to know just what we are assessing. If we are assessing portfolios that show responses to a variety of assignments from other instructors, we may not understand the context of some classes or the assumptions behind the particular work (although we might ask students to provide this information); we may also be evaluating the assignments as well as the responses, as better assignments tend to elicit better writing. The scoring of portfolios is particularly vexing for many reasons, including the variable quality of the components and the inherent complexity of the criteria.

The problem for teachers in using portfolios, then, is to maximize the advantages of this method of assessment while minimizing the disadvantages. Because portfolio assessment is so new in writing, we do not have long traditions of testing to rely on. This chapter will consider the advantages and disadvantages of portfolio assessment for different situations, with an eye to helping teachers avoid some of the problems that have emerged over the past few years. If you can perform this balancing act, you will find that portfolios are the most valuable means you have of combining evaluation with teaching.

TEACHER-GRADED CLASS PORTFOLIO

The easiest and most direct use of portfolios is in a single writing class. The student is expected to keep all drafts, revisions, and presentation copies in a folder as a record of the term's work. Some writing programs even design their own folders, sometimes with grading criteria and a decoder for marking symbols printed on them, and require every student to purchase one—a small moneymaker. The student brings the portfolio to conferences or to the writing center, and the final "exam" is to revise the most interesting papers in the portfolio and to write a self-assessment as a foreword to it.

Such a portfolio has important advantages for the student in a writing course. In the first place, the portfolio exemplifies the teacher's contention that writing is a process, not merely a product. Although the portfolio contains a series of products, as a whole it is evidence of the student's writing process. Some papers may be revised three or four times, in a good portfolio, and even the least talented writer will notice the changes from early drafts to presentation copies. Furthermore, the portfolio demonstrates that the student is really writing for the self, not just for the teacher or for the grade; almost all students take pride in the portfolio, want to preserve it at the end of the term, and are impressed at the quantity (if not the quality) of the work produced. If the portfolio includes, as it should, some in-class writing, revisions, and a self-assessment, it also protects students from the temptations of plagiarism; because the portfolio contains so much work that must be genuine, anything that is not is usually painfully evident to both student and teacher.

You have many options for assessing the portfolio. For example, you might focus on one or two papers with multiple revisions to give a "process grade" on the student's ability to improve from draft to draft; such a grade is a responsible way to reward effort by writers who have not yet learned to produce excellent final products. Perhaps that process grade can combine with grades on the products to give a fairer term grade than one based wholly on final drafts. Again, you might allow students to focus the portfolio on a few papers they like the best, or you might define the portfolio as including several essential papers, with their notes and drafts. The point is to promote student ownership of the portfolio, despite the fact that the teacher must finally grade the work, and to demonstrate that the writing grade depends on more than a finely edited product. Indeed, to drive that point home, some experienced instructors refuse to grade the portfolio at all, though that strikes me as an unfortunate loss of a powerful assessment tool.

Because the portfolio will probably include some writing in the process of revision, the terminology for student drafts calls for some thought. Many teachers will ask for a "first draft" and a "final draft" without clarifying what those terms mean. The teacher usually wants the first draft to be what the student thinks of as the final draft—an unedited but coherent piece of writing. The student usually thinks of the first draft as a rough set of notes (which might nonetheless be a useful record of getting under way for some portfolios). Because of these problems with terminology, I suggest using more precise terms. I like the term *zero draft* for the prose that comprises the notes, which, upon revision, then becomes a *discovery draft*. Almost always, this discovery draft then requires reorganization, focusing, and development. Typically, the discovery draft will not state its principal concept until the next-to-last paragraph; the student has discovered the real topic by writing about it. An experienced writer will realize this, throw away almost everything preceding that paragraph, and produce a new draft with that paragraph as the opening. But students usually feel it a waste to throw away anything and need the help and encouragement of a professional to see that the function of the discovery draft has been fulfilled if the writer has come to discover what he or she really wants to say.

The draft that revises the discovery draft will normally show the development and organization that a college paper needs, but this "final draft" is often much in need of editing. Some teachers will delay editing comments to this stage and, for a few selected papers, require a presentation copy with careful editing and a high degree of polish as a revision of the final draft.

But we do need to be careful to allow for different writing processes. Not every student—or every professional, for that matter—will follow this typical pattern. Some writers seem able to compose a series of initial drafts in their heads, and these writers turn out first drafts that need little revision; other writers may find that editing is the spur that leads to revision, rather than the tedious final cleanup stage of writing. Such exceptions—and they are rare— will define their writing process in special ways and are likely to need some flexibility if they are to meet a portfolio requirement for all stages of a particular writing task. The writing process is a concept, not a formula, and different writers, or the same writer on different occasions, may find a variety of routes to the finished paper.

The portfolio allows you to review—and perhaps grade—essays that have gone through a series of stages. If we do grade the various drafts, we should stay aware of the different purposes of the stages. The zero draft requires that the student collect thoughts, references, and experiences that stake out the area for the paper. The discovery draft revises the zero draft with the goal of finding out what is really interesting and worth saying about the area. The final draft focuses and develops that idea as fully as time and talent allow. The presentation draft revises the final draft for a demanding audience that expects the developed, interesting idea to be written with standard sentence structure, spelling, punctu- ation, and footnote form and appropriate control of tone, metaphor, and diction.

Though every paper in the portfolio need not include these stages (or other possible stages in a variety of writing processes), the portfolio is the only assessment device that can evaluate a student's ability to understand revision processes. We may talk about revision, but portfolio assessment supports that talk by collecting and evaluating several papers in multiple drafts. If the portfolio were to include only a collection of final drafts, this opportunity to support teaching about the writing process with assessment would be lost. And the great virtue of portfolio assessment is that it can document the revisions that show the essential learning about the writing process that goes on in the writing course, in a single folder at the end of the term.

To be sure, the improvement in teaching and learning that portfolios bring about can weigh heavily on the instructor. Course portfolios do leave you with a great heap of folders to get through at the end of the term. But no one demands that you read every word of every draft of every paper of every portfolio. You must read selectively, and since by this time you have come to know the students fairly well, you can decide where to invest your limited time. This is not cheating; the portfolios are part of the course, prepared so that the student will have a record of work to be proud of. "Did I really write all this?" a typical student will ask, with some bemusement. "You sure did," you and the portfolio will reply. "And some of it is really good, better than anything you have done before. Take it home and be proud of it."

STAFF-GRADED COURSE PORTFOLIO

Recognizing the value of portfolio assessment, some colleges have used it for assessment outside of the individual classroom. A typical example is the assessment of student portfolios from the writing class by faculty who have not taught the students' writing class. Students prepare portfolios for evaluation, following certain criteria (which I will address in a moment), and present the portfolios to an assessment team. The team might be as simple as the course instructor and one outsider or as elaborate as a full-fledged review board. This team then evaluates the portfolios, and that evaluation will play an important (perhaps even predominant) part in determining the students' grades.

This procedure has several clear advantages. The most important one is that the class teacher is relieved of full responsibility for grading. This is a definite plus, for if the portfolio is to be graded by others, the teacher then becomes more a coach than a judge. The teacher will in that case be helping the student prepare the best portfolio possible for the assessment that is to come. The student comes to see the teacher as a supporter rather than as an adversary, and the standards for judgment of the portfolio become a subject that the student wants to learn. The teacher's comments and grades become valuable clues to the way others like the teacher will probably grade the portfolio. Rather than giving a failing grade, for example, the teacher can merely indicate that a portfolio with papers of this quality, in his or her experience, will not pass. Any system that turns the teacher into a valued coach is likely to assist in student learning and, incidentally, make the teacher's life much more pleasant.

Students will sometimes find the unknown portfolio team even more threatening than the known course instructor and resist team grading; everyone is likely to be suspicious of outside evaluators, naturally enough. And some teachers may initially be uneasy about losing some of their power of assessment. If the assessment team works in secret and if the results are handed down as law without appeal, these concerns will grow and eventually undermine the entire portfolio plan. But if the staff work together to define the portfolios and the grading standards and the assessment gains the assent of the teachers, they will find the operation supportive rather than threatening. And once the staff see the portfolio assessment team as "us" rather than "them," they can allay student concerns by their confidence in and support of the grading standards. The persons responsible for the portfolio team must carefully and regularly consider ways to maintain the genuine collegiality of the program.

Further, the imposition of a staff grade for portfolios can set standards that reflect the institution rather than the individual teacher. Though most writing programs make attempts to normalize standards, few are able to do more than influence slightly how teachers grade. Every student knows that some teachers are hard, others easy, and the rest in-between. But with portfolio grading, those unjust differences are evened out somewhat, for everyone works to achieve fair and consistent grading of the portfolios, whoever the class teacher may be. To be sure, some teachers will be more effective than others, putting their students at an advantage. But the enforcement of reliable standards for grading will help less effective teachers and their students improve, for all students will be subject to the same consistent and appropriate criteria.

Of course, that very impersonalization of standards is a disadvantage of staff grading, for it may also work some injustice in particular cases. Many instructors feel uncomfortable with grades given to their students by others, particularly by others who do not know the students they are grading. Perhaps the excellent student whose work dropped sharply in quality because of a divorce or a parent's death ought to be given special consideration. And perhaps the good work of the talented writer should not receive as high a grade as it appears to deserve because, as the teacher knows, a little revision from that student would have produced truly superior work. Every department contemplating portfolio team assessment will have to discuss and resolve the relationship between the team grade and the course grade. One way of dealing with it would be to make the portfolio grade a set percentage of the term grade, which would remain the responsibility of the class teacher. Another would be to ask the portfolio assessment team to give a pass/fail grade to the portfolio and leave the letter grade for the course to the teacher.

If composition staff decide to use an assessment team approach, a series of decisions will have to be made about ways to foster communication between the team and the teachers, as well as about procedures for scoring. The communication issue I leave to those who know the local situation, but five of the most prominent procedural issues are (1) content of the portfolio, (2) leaving the original grades and comments on portfolio contents or removing them, (3) scoring procedures, (4) criteria for scoring reliably, and (5) appeals procedures.

Content of the Portfolio

I mentioned earlier some possible components of class portfolios. When an assessment team is evaluating portfolios, the staff need to attend even more closely to portfolio content than the individual instructor does; the class situation usually makes clear what is important and what the grading expectations are, but as soon as we move out of the class context, these matters must be made explicit and put in writing. The number of items in the portfolios must be limited so that they can be read in a reasonable amount of time, but the papers must represent what matters for the course, as defined by the staff. What is to be included, and why? Before those questions can be answered, some decisions must be made about the purpose of the evaluation.

One such purpose might be to determine or strongly influence the student's grade in the course; the teacher might not be permitted to vary more than, say, one grade from the assessment team's portfolio grade. For the assessment team to be able to proceed, it must reflect the staff consensus about what determines a student's grade for the course. This consensus will shape the decision about the required content of the portfolio.

- Perhaps the portfolio should contain the first paper in several drafts, the last paper in several drafts, two examples of in-class writing, and a self-assessment.

- Perhaps the class teacher and the student could agree on the three best papers the student has written.

- Perhaps all that is needed is the research paper, including all notes and drafts.

- Or the team may want to see specific kinds of writing and to apply particular standards to that writing, so specific papers may be needed.

Whatever the grading and selection criteria, they must be written out well in advance and distributed to all students and faculty. A few sample or composite portfolios, exemplifying a variety of grades, should be available in the library to anyone interested (with suitable care for privacy issues).

Another purpose might be to evaluate the first-year course, or an entire curriculum, not individual students. How much writing is in fact being required, how is it being responded to, and what are the standards? For this purpose, the portfolios may have to be as complete as possible, but only a sample of them need be evaluated. Every student will file a full portfolio of all work done in the course, and an administrative assistant will randomly select a few from each class, concealing the instructors' names (unless everyone agrees otherwise), and the assessment team will read without preconceptions to find out what these portfolios indicate is going on in the course as a whole.

Still other purposes will require different definitions of what the portfolio must contain. The essential principles to keep in mind are the need to match the purposes of the assessment to the curriculum—what is actually being taught—and then to the portfolios and to be clear about just what is being measured. Remember, a portfolio is not a test; it is only a collection of materials. Those materials must be specified, and an evaluation procedure must then follow, if the operation is to make sense.

Leaving or Removing Grades and Comments

If the portfolio is to be used for the generation of some sort of new grade, it seems fair to remove all the comments and grades of the teacher or to include a copy of the original before the teacher responded to it. Otherwise, the new grade will surely be influenced by the original grade and by the comments written on the paper. However, two major problems must be confronted if the staff decide to do this. First, the clerical work is enormous, either in collecting unmarked originals or in erasing or obliterating what the original teacher wrote. Second, the assessment team will lose the expertness of the original comments, with their reflection of the class context and the details of the assignment. (The actual assignment as handed out is, of course, a necessary attachment to each paper, but it is often only a skeleton of the task in context.) For essays based on reading material, this expertness may be crucial, unless the assessment team members complete all the assigned reading themselves. If the course allows a wide range of reading materials, it may be impossible for the assessment team to know every piece of reading, and instructor comments may then be necessary.

A further issue arises if the teacher comments are left on the student papers: assessment of those comments themselves. Some assessment is inevitable, even if we try to avoid it; the quality of teacher comments is an important aspect of teaching, and readers will notice their colleagues' high-quality work or the reverse. But perhaps we should not avoid it, as so much time and work is represented by those comments. This added component of teacher evaluation strikes terror in the hearts of some teachers and makes them apprehensive about portfolios; conversely, the opportunity to be evaluated (and presumably rewarded) for a major teacher activity that has rarely been noticed seems to other teachers yet another positive aspect of this complex assessment.

Scoring Procedures

Experience with essay tests has shown that reliable readings can take place only in controlled sessions, with all readers reading at the same time and place, under the direction of a chief reader. This experience may not hold true for portfolios (they are still relatively untried for assessment in writing), but it probably will, as the scoring of portfolios seems in every way even more difficult than the scoring of essays. The portfolio programs reporting consistent scores at Miami University and the University of Michigan, for example, conduct controlled scoring sessions with scoring guides and sample portfolios. Hence, if the evaluation is to be consistent and therefore meaningful, careful planning of a scoring session will be necessary.

Such planning involves many details, including facilities, time management, funding, and personnel. Sample portfolios, illustrating different levels of performance, and scoring guides will have to be prepared in advance, for consistency training. Each portfolio should be read twice, with discrepant scores given a resolution reading. The size of the portfolios and the complexity of the scoring will determine how fast the reading can go; leaders of the reading should be sure to score a small sample in advance to make a reasonable estimate of the pace. For example, if readers can score five portfolios an hour, forty readers will require, after training, two hours to score two hundred portfolios twice.

Resist using informal procedures, such as parceling out the portfolios to faculty to take home and treat as they wish. Though that may seem less burdensome, it merely disguises the nature of the work and makes it unreliable. Sometimes it seems too much trouble to work for consistency in scoring, particularly when the results may be as crude as a pass/fail score. But unreliable results are unfair and unprofessional. Instead, we should seek funding to make a controlled reading as pleasant and as rewarding as possible. Evaluation worth doing is worth doing well, which means in a fair way that gives dependable results.

Criteria for Scoring Reliably

Again, the experience of essay testing suggests that considerable effort will be required to get all readers to use the same scoring criteria. In addition to developing a scoring guide that is responsive both to the goals of the assessment and to the students and to compiling sample portfolios to illustrate the points on the scoring guide, one more step is needed: deciding on the weighting of the various components of the portfolio. Are the same criteria to be applied to first-draft, in-class writing as to a research paper that has gone through multiple drafts? If not—and good sense suggests not—how are the criteria to be applied?

Though these are difficult problems, they are manageable as long as they are dealt with in advance. Composition staff working together to decide the purpose, then the content, and then the scoring criteria for portfolios are really deciding on the meaning and standards for the composition course, a most worthwhile activity.

Sample portfolio scoring guides are usually available from well-developed programs, such as the ones described by Belanoff and Dickson. For the portfolio scoring guide used by Miami University to decide which entering students may be exempted from first-year composition, see Daiker and colleagues or White in the Selected References at the end of this chapter.

Appeals Procedure

If the portfolio evaluators will be making grade or advancement decisions, some appeals procedure will be necessary. As with any other kind of assessment, portfolio assessment is not perfect, and some mistakes will be made. If the assessment team hands down a grade that a student, perhaps backed by the instructor, feels to be wrong, the case must be heard. However, because portfolio assessment tends to be so time-consuming, it is a good idea to think through in advance just how appeals can be minimized and handled expeditiously.

The most effective way to minimize appeals is to develop a demonstrably careful and reliable method of scoring. A simple description of the complex and expensive scoring mechanism will sometimes make the student realize that the scoring decision was made with care. A requirement for a written statement of appeal will discourage frivolous requests, and a requirement for evidence of procedural or other error for an appeal to be heard will reduce requests to the truly serious ones. When the appeals board reviews the portfolio, it needs to reestablish the context of the original scoring, using the same scoring guide and sample portfolios at the various score levels. Too many appeals will choke the system; more than an occasional one is a sign that insufficient care and groundwork have gone into the program.

A final note on the assessment team approach to portfolios for the composition course: Even if the focus is on individual student scores, try to find ways to use the portfolios for program assessment as well. Perhaps, after the scoring session is completed, a half hour reflecting on what the students are learning, or might be learning, would be more productive than any series of staff meetings dealing with the subject in the abstract.

PORTFOLIOS FOR BARRIER ASSESSMENTS

As Chapter 5 described them, barrier assessments serve as hurdles: Students must get over them if they are to continue toward the degree. Increasingly, portfolios are replacing multiple-choice and essay tests in barrier assessments because they give a more complete and, usually, more accurate picture of a student's writing ability.

The major difference between barrier assessments and other kinds of evaluation is the extremely high stakes involved. A student who does not pass the barrier may not proceed, regardless of other abilities, course grades, or teacher recommendations. The nature of the barrier puts great pressure on the assessment: Because it essentially deprives some students of their property rights in their education, it must meet the highest standards of validity and reliability. For these reasons, typically, the passing score on barrier assessments tends to be very low; if only the grossest incompetence fails, court action is less likely.

Nonetheless, the logic of the barrier assessment is reasonable enough: If the student cannot read or write at a minimum level, upper-division work is sure to lead to failure, and graduation from a college would be farcical. The student's progress to the degree should be held up until reading and writing are adequate.

But as this ideal enters practice, many problems develop. For example, shouldn't minimum proficiency be a matter of entrance requirements, not midstream barrier tests? And what do we say of students with many high grades, even in upper-division courses, who fail the barrier assessment? What about talented students in some fields, such as mathematics or music, who may be weak at verbal skills? And what do we do about students from non-

English-speaking homes or from homes with variant dialects of English who are nonetheless succeeding in their course work?

Portfolios naturally solve many of these problems, for by their very nature they demonstrate writing and thinking in a school and course context, rather than in isolation as a test does. Many students who cannot pass a timed writing test can still turn in written work that, after due revision, will meet reasonable standards. Hence, many campuses that feel the need for barrier assessments of students but find the contradictions and practical difficulties of conventional tests for this purpose more than they want to encounter are considering using portfolio barrier assessments.

It is beyond the scope of this book to pursue portfolio assessment into this kind of universitywide assessment in detail. But we should note that as the scope and stakes of the assessment expand, its implementation difficulties do also. As we went from the relative ease of the single class portfolio assessment to the much greater complexity of the course assessment team, the problems expanded greatly. As we move to school or university assessments, the problems increase again. For example, when faculty assessment teams start scoring writing outside of their fields of training, they lose some of their professional authority. How do we score papers written in a discourse community we may know nothing about? How can we grade analyses of books we have not read, written for contexts we do not share?

Essay tests used for barrier assessment are subject to the same questions, but the tests are normally written to a single text or question, so an assessment team can develop special expertness for the scoring. Portfolio assessments lack such controls; indeed, their particular virtue is that they are free from such limitations. But that very freedom makes their use for barrier testing more risky.

As composition programs gain practical experience with portfolio assessment, they are likely to be asked to make larger uses of portfolios for the university. This prospect should be approached with caution, even as it opens new possibilities for context-sensitive and increasingly valid writing assessment.

SOME MODEL PORTFOLIO PROGRAMS

Interest in portfolios for the assessment of writing has begun to show up in the journals and on the bookshelves. In almost all cases, the published material is based on a portfolio project on a particular campus. The four books with *portfolio* in their titles in the Selected References at the end of this chapter were the first to appear. Yancey's book is a collection of essays by various hands, all focused on classroom uses of portfolios. The Belanoff and Dickson collection includes examples of a variety of portfolio uses at a wide range of colleges and universities. The collection of essays edited by Laurel Black and colleagues focuses on the theoretical as well as practical issues of portfolio assessment. The monograph edited by Donald Daiker and associates focuses specifically on the Miami University program, which allows entering students to present portfolios for assessment in an attempt to gain equivalency credit for freshman English. The articles by Elbow and Belanoff and by Roemer and colleagues present details about the use of portfolios as an exit assessment for freshman composition at the State University of New York and the University of Cincinnati, respectively.

Like most educational innovations, portfolio assessment in writing has been spreading by word of mouth and through conference presentations. The educators and scholars involved in portfolio projects are usually willing, even eager, to respond to queries or to visitors; faculty contemplating a portfolio project should consult the sources I have listed and their authors. Some other programs taking fresh approaches to portfolio assessment are at New Mexico State University (Chris Burnham), the University of Alaska, Southeast (Joey Waters), the University of Michigan (William Condon), and Washington State University (Susan Wyche-Smith). The Washington State experiment is particularly interesting because it will be operating on a very large scale and combines an essay test (as a screening device) with portfolios so that only a small percentage of the submitted portfolios will need to be evaluated.

Research on portfolios is proceeding much more slowly than practice. The article by Hamp-Lyons and Condon shows that this research has now moved beyond the enthusiastic show-and-tell phase into serious examination of the problems posed by this attractive assessment device.

PORTFOLIOS IN THE FUTURE

Finally, I must stress that the advantages of portfolios, great as they are, seem at present to be balanced by a series of problems that may or may not be manageable. Of all the problems described in this chapter, none is more resistant than the time burden that portfolio reading places on teachers already overburdened with too many classes with too many students. Nonetheless, portfolios may well be the wave of the future in writing assessment.

Scores of campuses and hundreds of faculty are already engaged in portfolio experimentation. Granting agencies are funding portfolio projects for freshman placement, for general education outcomes, and for numbers of other purposes. The energy and resources furthering portfolio assessment remind me of the surge in interest in essay testing that occurred two decades ago, an outpouring of creativity that coped with problems of reliability and validity that seemed insurmountable at the time.

One of these portfolio experimenters, alluding to literary theory, told me that she favored portfolio assessment because it was "a deconstruction of assessment itself." That is, portfolios disallow the too easy reduction of assessment to tests and then to test scores for the sorting of students; they also disallow the reduction of all writing to first-draft exposition, insisting by definition that many different kinds of writing are valuable. Portfolios cannot be reduced to tests, nor can the deep humanity of students' writing, feeling, and thinking be removed from portfolios—that creative unmanageability is both their strength and their weakness. If portfolios do become the standard method of evaluating writing, we will be assured that writing itself remains valued, taught, and delightfully unpredictable. We will also know that education remains a matter of thinking and creativity, despite all the forces that drive colleges toward mass measures of information processing. But before this can occur, we will have to learn how to handle this new assessment device with care, fairness, economy, and responsibility.

SELECTED REFERENCES

Belanoff, Pat, and Marcia Dickson. *Portfolios: Process and Product.* Portsmouth, NH: Boynton/Cook, 1991.

Black, Laurel, Donald A. Daiker, Jeffrey Sommers, and Gail Stygall. *New Directions in Portfolio Assessment: Reflective Practice, Critical Theory, and Large-Scale Scoring.* Portsmouth, NH: Boynton/Cook, 1994.

Daiker, Donald A., Jeffrey Sommers, Gail Stygall, and Laurel Black. *The Best of Miami's Portfolios.* Oxford, OH: Miami University Department of English, 1990–1993.

Elbow, Peter, and Pat Belanoff. "Portfolios as a Substitute for Proficiency Examinations." *CCC* 37 (1986): 336–39.

Hamp-Lyons, Liz, and William Condon. "Questioning Assumptions about Portfolio-based Assessment." *CCC* 44 (1993): 176–90.

Roemer, Marjorie, Lucille M. Schulz, and Russel K. Durst. "Portfolios and the Process of Change." *CCC* 42 (1991): 455–69.

White, Edward M. "Organizing and Managing Holistic Essay or Portfolio Readings." *Teaching and Assessing Writing: Recent Advances in Understanding, Evaluating, and Improving Student Performance.* 2nd ed. San Francisco: Jossey-Bass, 1994. 197–217.

———. "Resource B: Submission Guidelines and Scoring Guide for Portfolios." *Teaching and Assessing Writing: Recent Advances in Understanding, Evaluating, and Improving Student Performance.* 2nd ed. San Francisco: Jossey-Bass, 1994. 300–03.

Yancey, K. *Portfolios in the Writing Classroom.* Urbana, IL: National Council of Teachers of English, 1992.

CONCLUDING NOTES ON ASSESSMENT AND THE TEACHING OF WRITING

————————— ⟨⟩ —————————

This book provides many writing assignments along with much practical advice on teaching, responding to, and assessing writing. One might think that it ought also to provide ready materials for reliable pretesting and posttesting of students, to allow statistically significant demonstration that they have improved in writing skill over the course of study. The essay topics in Chapters 3 and 4 might actually be used for that purpose. But we should note that the sample writing assignments in Chapter 1 more accurately represent the complexity of the world of writing instruction than the pre-/posttesting models do.

Earlier editions of this book included parallel forms of a multiple-choice test, which examined only one aspect of the writing process (editing) and assumed that editing skills will improve as writing improves. The evidence for such an assumption is skimpy (see George Hillocks, *Research on Written Composition*, Urbana, IL: National Council of Teachers of English, 1986) and uncertain, particularly for racial and ethnic minorities. This edition drops those tests, and most writing teachers (familiar with earlier editions or not) will sigh with relief that they are gone. The essay tests examine much more of the construct "writing ability" but still omit much that is taught in the writing course: drafting, revision, development of complex ideas, and use of sources,

165

for example. In addition, the composition course ought also to teach some matters that almost never appear on writing tests: use of the dictionary and the complex meanings of words, ability to cope with ambiguity of ideas, understanding of complicated reading, even a love of reading, thinking, and writing for their own sake.

In short, ironic as it may seem, this book, which began as an evaluation manual, is in part designed to argue against simple uses of evaluation to trivialize the composition course. Wherever I have included an assessment device or a scoring guide, I have tried to hedge it with cautions, warn of its limitations, and guard against its misuse. The assignments in Chapter 1 show the broad range of advanced skills that college composition courses teach, and they demonstrate the great complexity of evaluation involved in responding usefully to student writing. No one should imagine that the writing assessments included here (or those used anywhere) measure more than they do; nor should the concern for measurable outcomes reduce the composition course to a mere matter of editing, just because editing is relatively easy to test. Assessment is immensely useful for teaching and is certainly worth much more attention than it has usually gotten from composition teachers. A good composition course always involves regular evaluation of student work. But as I have pointed out, the misuse of assessment is a serious problem in American education. The student who has moved from some ability to handle the first personal experience essay in Chapter 3 to competency at handling the research paper assignment given at the end of Chapter 1 has made immense progress in a vast range of thinking, reading, and writing skills. Most composition courses in fact do bring students some distance along these largely uncharted paths. Assessment in composition should support this complex and difficult job: Assessment should help students and teachers see how far they have come and how far they need to go without diminishing the adventure of the journey.

INDEX

167